In today's healthcare environment, the two most frustrated parties are the physician and the patient - the only two entities that are required for a healthcare transaction!

Dr. Grace Torres-Hodges opens a door that has been quietly and surreptitiously shut over the past few decades, namely, a physician's awareness and choice to enter independent practice.

Matt Ohrt, Executive Director
Free Market Medical Association

EARLY PRAISE FROM PHYSICIANS AT EVERY CAREER STAGE

Doctor Do, Doctor Don't is essential reading for medical students and residents. Dr. Grace Torres-Hodges' book will guide new physicians step by step on how to choose the style of medical practice that best suits them while also serving as an anecdote to a system that encourages physician passivity and compliance. This book will not only help new medical school graduates settle into a practice they can love, it may help bring about a new generation of physician leaders willing to help improve the entire healthcare system. It should be part of every physician-in-training's curriculum.

Gregg Stefanek, DO
Physician, TedX speaker, and healthcare consultant

Timely. Poignant. *Doctor Do, Doctor Don't* pulls the curtain back on the "other side" of medicine for the early career physician. Dr. Grace Torres-Hodges' delivery is honest, raw, informative, and provocative. This should be mandatory reading before any physician signs a contract.

Todd Otten, MD
Physician, co-author of *Ripple of Change,*
and executive producer of *Suck It Up, Buttercup*

Doctor Do, Doctor Don't by Grace Torres-Hodges is a must-read blueprint for medical students, residents, early-career physicians, and any doctor considering a career transition. Packed with pragmatic, highly actionable guidance on compensation, practice models, and common pitfalls, it provides the real-world insights physicians need to make informed career decisions with confidence.

Rebekah Bernard, MD
Physician, speaker, and author of *How to Be a Rockstar Doctor*

The transition from the classroom to the actual healthcare system is incredibly overwhelming. This book gives future doctors the contract confidence and financial literacy we actually need to take control of our careers from day one.

A.A.
MS-3 MD candidate

Drawing on her experience navigating the corporate healthcare world after residency, Dr. Torres-Hodges shares the essential concepts every young physician needs to hear before starting their career. This is the book every young physician should read, annotate, and then discuss with seasoned colleagues. It builds the foundation for a healthy, sustainable relationship with both clinical medicine and one's personal life. When so much of the conversation around healthcare feels discouraging, *Doctor Do, Doctor Don't* reminds young physicians that a rewarding, well-informed career in medicine is absolutely within reach.

Aaron Morgenstein, MD
Orthopedic Surgeon and co-founder, *FlexMedStaff*

As a fourth-year medical student standing right at the edge of everything this book covers, *Doctor Do, Doctor Don't* is the resource I have always been looking for. I finally have the expert guidance I needed to navigate the parts of medicine nobody teaches you — and I feel far more confident about my path because of it.

J.B.
MS-4 DPM candidate

The concepts presented here are not complicated, but as every physician knows, simple does not always mean easy. *Doctor Do, Doctor Don't* provides an honest roadmap from someone who understands both the opportunities and the obstacles. I recommend it to any physician who wants to build a career on their own terms while preserving the values that drew them to medicine in the first place.

Brittany Busse, MD
Physician / Founder, ViTel Health Physician Services Cooperative and Executive Director of Women's Health, Velocity Health Clinic

Entering the medical field today can feel overwhelming, but Dr. Grace Torres-Hodges offers a beautifully supportive beacon of light. *Doctor Do, Doctor Don't* is packed with incredibly useful advice, delivered in her signature-style, gentle, pleasant and informative. It doesn't just prepare newly minted doctors for the logistics of practice—it provides a focus on physician values and an emotional scaffolding they need to thrive in this brave new world.

Raymond Kordonowy, MD
Physician and Owner of ILMWP

Dr. Grace Torres-Hodges writes with the credibility of a practicing physician and the clarity of someone who actually wants you to understand what you're signing up for. Read it before your first contract, not after.

Jim McDannald, DPM
Owner of *PodiatryGrowth.com* and co-host of *Podiatry Marketing podcast*

Medicine asks medical professionals to care deeply for others. Dr. Grace Torres-Hodges' work reminds us that protecting the integrity of our own careers is part of that responsibility.

Dana Coriel, MD
Physician, author, serial-entrepreneur, and founder of *SoMeDocs*

Students enter medical school with an open mind and a deep hunger for knowledge, eager to begin their career of caring for people. This book has the power to convince students that they don't have to abandon their dream of providing quality medical care and convince them to say "no" to the sick system and "yes" to their sick patients by becoming independent physicians. Dr. Grace not only imparts valuable knowledge about how to operate as an independent practitioner, but she also has a gift for instilling confidence. Every medical student needs to read this book. It will change your life and thereby change the life of every patient you treat.

J.L.
MS-4 MD/PhD candidate

With healthcare becoming more of a business and less about the best interest of patient/doctor relationship, it is proving to be difficult to hold true to our values and why we went into medicine. As an attending physician who spends much time with students, residents and fellows, I look forward to sharing this book with all of them to help guide the future of our profession in making some of the most important decisions of their life.

Melissa Shukla, DPM, FACFAS
Podiatric Surgery and Wound Care

Dr. Torres-Hodges has written a book in defense of the interests of the one group that is not used to thinking about its own interests – aspiring physicians. This book should be required reading for all medical students and residents.

Sonny Morton, MD, MBA/MHA
Board of Directors, *Benjamin Rush Institute*

DOCTOR DO, DOCTOR ~~DON'T~~

Actionable Dos/Don'ts for Navigating Pay, Practice Models, and Pitfalls

GRACE TORRES-HODGES, DPM, MBA

EDITED BY SUSAN J. PATNAIK

Doctor Do, Doctor Don't: Actionable Dos/Don'ts for Navigating Pay, Practice Models, and Pitfalls

Edited by Susan J. Patnaik
ISBN-13: 979-8-9891707-4-6 (Paperback)
ISBN-13: 979-8-9891707-5-3 (Electronic Book)
ISBN-13: 979-8-9891707-6-0 (Audiobook)

DEDICATION

To the next generation of doctors—

May you enter this profession with eyes wide open and with true informed consent. Take note of the system you are stepping into, protect your autonomy, and keep your first loyalty where it belongs: to your patients, and to the integrity of your calling.

CONTENTS

FOREWORD

Young physicians are entering the field of medicine at one of the most challenging moments in modern history.

Many began their training with a calling to heal, serve patients, and practice medicine with compassion and independence. Yet they are graduating into a healthcare system burdened by bureaucracy, administrative complexity, and increasingly large and centralized healthcare organizations.

Physicians today face mounting pressures from insurers, regulators, hospital systems, and reimbursement structures that often place productivity metrics and compliance burdens ahead of the doctor-patient relationship.

So it's hardly a surprise that rates of physician burnout and dissatisfaction with the field continue to rise. Too many doctors feel they have lost control over how they practice medicine, how they spend their time, and how their careers are unfolding.

The profession physicians entered decades ago is not the same profession today's graduates are inheriting.

Independent physician practice used to be the norm. For generations, physicians largely controlled the terms under which they practiced medicine. They owned practices, made staffing decisions, negotiated directly with patients and payors, and exercised broad discretion over clinical care.

Today's physicians operate in a far different environment, one increasingly characterized by large institutions, complex re-

imbursement systems, and layers of administrative oversight. Most physicians now begin their careers as employees of large organizations. That's not inherently bad. But it has created challenges and tradeoffs that young physicians deserve to understand before they sign their first contract.

Most physicians receive little preparation for these realities during their medical training. Dr. Grace Torres-Hodges understands the consequences of that gap. This book is her response -- a practical and thoughtful guide for physicians seeking to navigate today's healthcare system with clarity, purpose, and a deeper understanding of the forces shaping modern medicine.

Dr. Torres-Hodges understands something many policymakers and administrators too often overlook. Physicians are not merely employees within the healthcare system. They are highly-trained caregivers entrusted with extraordinary responsibility. They have a duty to exercise sound clinical judgment on behalf of their patients.

Protecting physicians' ability to exercise that judgment is essential not only for physicians but for the patients who rely on them.

When physicians lose the ability to exercise independent judgment, patients often lose as well. Medical care works best when treatment decisions are guided by the needs of individual patients rather than administrative mandates, reimbursement formulas, or institutional priorities. A healthcare system that reduces physicians to technicians carrying out directives from insurers, regulators, or corporate managers risks weakening the very relationships that make effective care possible.

Preserving physician autonomy is therefore not simply a professional concern. It is a patient-care imperative.

Throughout these pages, readers will find candid discussions on topics ranging from employment contracts and compensation models to burnout, financial literacy, insurance systems, and career design. Readers are encouraged not simply to re-

act to the system around them but to think carefully about the careers they want to build and the professional values they hope to preserve.

It's a timely message given the pressures physicians face today. I have spent much of my career examining these challenges from a public-policy perspective. In that work, I have come to appreciate how regulations, payment systems, subsidies, and market distortions can affect the delivery and cost of care.

Dr. Torres-Hodges approaches these challenges from the perspective of a practicing clinician who has experienced many of them firsthand. Nevertheless, our underlying concerns are the same. When policy weakens competition, rewards consolidation, or empowers third parties to interfere with medical decision-making, physicians and patients feel the consequences every day.

In recent years, consolidation among hospitals and insurers -- often reinforced by government policy -- has transformed the practice of medicine.

Administrative burdens consume hours that could otherwise be devoted to patient care. Prior authorization requirements, reimbursement pressures, and compliance demands interfere with clinical decision-making and create frustration on both sides of the exam room.

Taken together, these forces make it easier for physicians to trade independent practice for the apparent convenience and security of employed practice without fully recognizing the long-term consequences of that tradeoff.

The book you are holding provides both the perspective and practical guidance that new physicians need to navigate this environment with a clear understanding of the opportunities and challenges ahead. It does this not through a message of cynicism or despair but one of empowerment.

As Dr. Torres-Hodges makes clear, there are many ways to build a fulfilling career in medicine, even today. Physicians can still preserve their values, maintain meaningful relationships with patients, and create professional lives aligned with their principles. But doing so requires practical wisdom, knowledge, and courage.

At its core, Doctor Do, Doctor Don't is a book about intentionality. It reminds physicians that careers do not simply happen to them. The choices they make about employment, compensation, finances, contracts, and practice models will shape not only their professional satisfaction but also their ability to serve patients effectively.

Those decisions often seem technical or financial in nature. But they ultimately influence how much time physicians spend with patients, how much control they retain over clinical decisions, and how sustainable their careers become over the long term.

Whether a physician chooses private practice, employment, academics, entrepreneurship, or some combination of these paths, Dr. Torres-Hodges encourages them to make those decisions thoughtfully and with a clear understanding of the trade-offs involved.

The future of American medicine will depend not only on scientific breakthroughs or the direction of public policy but on whether physicians retain the judgment, professional independence, and commitment to patients that have long defined the profession. Dr. Torres-Hodges has written a thoughtful and timely guide for those determined to do exactly that.

Sally C. Pipes
President, CEO, and Thomas W. Smith Fellow in Health Care Policy
Pacific Research Institute

INTRODUCTION

I remember standing where you are now — somewhere between "I can't believe I made it this far" and "I hope this is all going to be worth it." You've survived exams, call, evaluations, and more sleepless nights than you can count. You've earned your place in this profession, and I'm genuinely glad you chose medicine.

For generations, becoming a doctor has been considered a pinnacle of success. It has offered a stable, respected career, rich with intellectual challenge, high earning potential, and the privilege of caring for people at their most vulnerable. Few occupations compare. My hope is that you will experience that same professional and personal fulfillment in your own career.

But there is something I need to tell you — something I wish someone had told me more clearly when I was in your shoes.

The career path you are stepping into is not the same one your attendings trained for, and it is certainly not the one physicians enjoyed a generation or two ago. The ground under our feet has been shifting for years — sometimes slowly, sometimes abruptly — and many of us in practice have had to find our bearings the hard way.

The advantages of a medical career still exist, but doctors today face challenges their predecessors never imagined. The dynamics of providing healthcare have changed in ways that constrain physicians. Until recently, most doctors maintained a great deal of autonomy over their practice, and patient care clearly ruled the day. Neither can be taken for granted anymore.

As a result, physicians are reporting higher levels of dissatisfaction with their careers than ever before. An unsettling number are leaving the profession altogether. Some have even succumbed to despair so deep it led to suicide. I don't share this to be dramatic. I share it because I don't want you to become another quiet casualty of a system you were never taught to navigate.

You might be wondering why not many people have told you any of this.

Good question!

It is hard for people to talk about what they don't fully understand. Many of the changes reshaping healthcare come "from on high" — from institutions and boardrooms far removed from the exam room and the operating room. They are communicated to physicians in polished, strategic language that softens their true impact, at least at first. These changes have, in a sense, snuck up on us while we were busy caring for patients.

Most physicians can feel that the profession has changed. They sense the difference in their day-to-day experience, even if they cannot fully explain how and why. Many are already deeply entrenched in their careers, with financial obligations, family responsibilities, and contracts that are hard to unwind. They don't see obvious solutions. So, they say nothing.

That is why I lecture on this topic, and why I wrote this book. From where I stand in practice, it feels important to say out loud what often goes unspoken in training. Every new physician deserves to read the fine print on the career they have chosen.

I am not here to cast doubt on your decision to become a doctor. I am here to encourage you to pursue your dreams of practicing medicine — wisely. My goal is to help you enter this profession informed about the system you are about to become part of and prepared to build a career that supports your personal and professional well-being. No one wants to see physicians leaving medicine, or worse. It is not good for them, it is not good for the profession, and it is not good for society.

Like many physicians, I've felt the impact of how medicine has changed, and unlike my younger self, I've spent more than a decade digging into the "why" behind it — struggling with these questions, talking them through with colleagues, and testing solutions in my own practice. Along the way, I even wrote a book about what I learned: *Private Practice Solution.* While writing that book, I uncovered concrete ways physicians can take greater control of their careers, particularly at the outset when those early decisions shape so much of what follows.

You may not realize it yet, but the choices you make in the next few years — about jobs, contracts, practice models, and money — will quietly dictate many aspects of your professional experience down the road. My intention here is to help you understand the practical realities of the profession you are about to enter: the good, the bad, and the unexpected. More importantly, I want you to understand the choices you have ahead of you (and the consequences of those choices), so you can choose wisely — so that you can, in effect, give informed consent for your own career. I'm sure you are familiar with that term.

Right now, you are spending years of your life learning how to care for and treat patients, how to resolve their medical issues, and how to save their lives. But now is also the time to learn how to care for your practice.

As a physician, your first patient should never be a person. Your first patient should be you — and by extension, your practice — by which I mean your career.

Think of the oxygen mask on the airplane: First you secure your own mask, then you help the person next to you. If you can't breathe, you can't help anyone else breathe. The same is true of your practice. If you don't take care of your practice, eventually, you might find you aren't able to care for others — at least not effectively.

Medical students and residents are taught that medicine is about judgment. I have long encouraged the medical students I work with to be like sponges and soak up as much information as they can during training. But I also remind them that practicing medicine requires more than rote memorization. It requires critical thinking. You are learning not only what to do in any given situation, but also what not to do. Good decisions are made only after getting a full picture, recognizing that there are choices, and considering all the options.

Ironically, when it comes to sending graduates out into the world, our training system often violates that very principle. These days, it seems it conditions doctors to follow a single path without ever questioning who drew the map.

That wasn't always the case. Over the years, I've watched the slow creep of this conditioning. I've experienced it firsthand in conversations. I always make a point of asking medical students and residents one simple question: "So, what are you going to do after residency?" It wasn't that long ago — well into the early 2000s — that the majority would tell me, without hesitation, that they planned to hang a shingle and start their own private practice.

With each passing year, however, I began hearing that response less and less.

The shift in thinking among medical graduates has been seismic. Today, many residents tell me they are signing on for employment with one of the following: a hospital system, an insurance company, a private equity–backed medical group, an academic medical center, a government agency, a physician staffing firm, or a retail or technology-enabled healthcare corporation.

It is almost as if the system is discouraging autonomy-minded thinking among young physicians by rewarding compliance at the outset of their careers. If physicians are serious about preserving the integrity of medicine and the medical profession, rising doctors need to be informed early on that you have choices when it comes to building your career — and that those choices need not be scary.

Autonomy isn't anti-establishment. Autonomy is the antidote to institutional dependency.

The longer medical students and residents are trained to conform without question, the greater the loss will be — for there will be fewer doctors who remember that medicine was once a calling, not a compliance exercise.

A vast healthcare system awaits you beyond the walls of the hospital where you are now training. It is made up of many different stakeholders, each with their own vested interests. It is complicated, political, and governed by forces largely foreign to you at this stage. I understand if you haven't given it much thought. Your mind can't be everywhere at once, and your first day as a fully licensed attending may still feel like a distant point on the horizon.

But every physician practicing today will tell you: That day comes much more quickly than you expect, and now is the time to plan ahead and prepare for it. Many will also tell you they wish someone had handed them a book like this one when they were in your shoes.

Here is the good news: Your skills as a doctor are all the leverage you will need to build a career that supports your interests and well-being. You must not lose sight of this fact. The ball is, in many ways, in your court. In the pages ahead, I aim to show you how to use your skill set to design a career in which you feel valued, respected, and true to yourself.

So, what exactly do you need to know about the practicalities of a career in medicine before you transition from physician-in-training to practicing physician? Quite a bit, to be honest. But don't worry — I will walk you through it step by step.

Section One, Getting Your House in Order, is about building a firm foundation of values, financial practices, and proper insurance coverage. Chapter One walks you through the importance of identifying your values before you begin building your career, so you can avoid painful misalignment down the road. Chapter Two offers a crash course in personal finance and stretching those first paychecks to cover your expenses while you begin tackling your loans. You'll learn how to calculate your take-home pay, plan for loan repayment, and build healthy habits around tracking, saving, and talking about money. Chapter Three wraps up the section with a discussion of insurance: the forms of coverage you will need as a practicing physician and key considerations for each.

Section Two, How the System Actually Works, pulls back the curtain on the structures you'll be working within. It walks you through your employment options, highlights the tradeoffs of each, points out pitfalls to avoid, and explains different models of medical practice. Chapter Four clarifies the tradeoffs between employment and independent practice and introduces the possibility of hybrid models. Chapter Five helps you "follow the money" by introducing you to the various payors in healthcare and showing how their incentives shape your day-to-day reality. Chapter Six distinguishes reimbursement from compensation and helps you understand that, in the end, it's what you keep that counts.

Section Three, Career and Life on Your Terms, focuses on long-term satisfaction and sustainability in medicine. Burnout is a real danger for physicians, and you need to know how it can creep up on you and how to guard against it. Chapter Seven walks you through different practice models and invites you to choose your own adventure, rather than defaulting to the path of least resistance. Chapter Eight covers contracts and negotiation and encourages you to ask for what you need — because it really is worth asking. Chapter Nine explores burnout, boundaries, and becoming human again, offering tools for reclaiming your time and sense of self when necessary. Chapter Ten discusses leadership and growth, even if you're not officially "in charge," and shows how you can shape your environment and influence the culture around you.

This book is designed to bridge the gap between the medical training you are receiving now and the transition you will soon make into professional practice. It is meant to help you navigate the professional terrain ahead with a clear understanding of your options and the confidence to make decisions that align with your values and aspirations. It is also meant to help you think critically about your future and avoid the pitfalls that lead to burnout and discontentment.

Practicing medicine can be every bit as rewarding as you imagine — as long as you make wise professional choices along the way. The decisions you make about your career will shape how you show up for your patients and for yourself. You are your practice's first patient. Take care of this patient, and you will be able to take care of countless others.

SECTION ONE

GETTING YOUR HOUSE IN ORDER

CHAPTER ONE

IT STARTS WITH VALUES

The Non-Negotiables of Your Career

"Without character, a person becomes a puppet, led by the interests of others rather than their own values."
– Anonymous

Part 1: Your Values and Your "Why"

Can you imagine turning down fifty million dollars to avoid compromising your professional values?

The comedian Dave Chappelle can ... and did. He said he didn't want to make content he found distasteful, and that he felt uncomfortable with how the industry machine was treating him. So, in 2005, he broke his contract with Comedy Central and retreated to South Africa. For all he knew, he would never work again. At least, not at that level.

People called Chappelle crazy for turning down that much money. But he didn't feel crazy. In fact, he believed taking the money and compromising his values were what would make him feel crazy.

"I wasn't walking away from the money. I was walking away from the circumstances that would prevent me from making the kind of work that I want to make," Chappelle said.

Chappelle's actions clearly demonstrate the hierarchy of his values. He probably likes money just fine. Who doesn't? But he obviously values his creative freedom more than money. How do we know that? Because he demonstrated it with his actions.

How many people would make the same decision? Probably not many. Why? Because not too many people value creative autonomy to the extent that he does. That makes Chappelle a rarity in this world. Not because of the choice he made, but because of the personal integrity that compelled that choice.

You may never be offered fifty million dollars to do something that clashes with your values, but you will be offered jobs, contracts, schedules, and "opportunities" that quietly ask you to trade away pieces of what matters to you. Some of them will even come wrapped in language that sounds virtuous, patient-centered, and "aligned with your values" on paper. That's why it's so important to know what you stand for before the offer is on the table.

Your values are on display every minute of every day in the form of what you do or refrain from doing: how you spend your time, how you spend your money, the company you keep, the sacrifices you make, the commitments you uphold.

In this chapter, I want to challenge you to reflect upon your values — your personal values as well as professional values — and consider that you, like Chappelle, might be a rarity in this world. I want to give you credit for that. And I want you to take credit for it as well.

You might be wondering why I'm asking you to do that. This is a book about transitioning from medical school and residency to practicing medicine. Why all the questions about my values?

Simple. You've only ever experienced the medical profession as a student from the bleachers, ready and eager to get in the game. You are idealistic and gung ho. At the moment, your values align perfectly with the values of the system you are part of. It's all about providing the best care for the patient. In your capacity as a student or resident, you are sheltered from administrative practicalities. So, at this stage, you are unfamiliar with all the various pressures you will experience in the profession once you graduate. And as a result, you might well take it for granted that everyone you interact with throughout your career will share your value system.

Please don't think I am calling you naive. I'm only saying that you've been trained in a vacuum, under ideal circumstances, without the outside forces of the system bearing down on you. It is only natural and right for you to be full of idealism. It's where all doctors start out. Without idealism and optimism there would be no future doctors.

Let's look at a choice you made recently and consider the trade-offs inherent in that choice and what they indicate about your values. Not too long ago, you decided to go to medical school. You filled out the applications. You took the MCAT. You either arranged a loan or you emptied your bank account. And then you showed up and did the work. Did you ever stop and consider what you traded off when you made that decision and took those actions? Did you ever stop and consider what that decision reveals about your personal and professional values?

Instead of going to medical school and pursuing a career in medicine ...

- You could have gone to law school. Trade-off – a career in law.
- You could have taken a job on Wall Street. Trade-off – a career in finance.
- You could have taken the tuition money and invested it in the stock market. Tradeoff – the thrill of financial speculation and potential payoff.
- You could have hiked the Appalachian Trail. Tradeoff – a spiritual experience in the woods.
- You could have sailed around the world and learned new languages. Tradeoff – a cultural experience at sea.

Some people might call you crazy for having decided to go to medical school instead of pursuing one of the other options. Just like people called Chappelle crazy.

But, then again, not everyone shares your values.

By choosing to go to medical school, you demonstrated that you value things like:

- Academic and professional achievement
- Scientific knowledge
- Hard work
- Solving problems
- Serving others
- Future security

What other values can you add to that list? What other tradeoffs were inherent in your decision? Answering questions like these is the beginning of defining your personal "why" for pursuing a career in medicine — the beginning of consciously naming and claiming your personal and professional values.

Pursuing a medical degree has not been a walk in the park. I know; I've been there. You've sacrificed your time, your money, your sleep, maybe even some relationships in exchange for becoming a physician. But you have made peace with that. Why? Because what you are getting is more valuable to you than what you are giving up.

Did you actually ever go through the exercise of debating the tradeoffs with yourself like this? Did you do this before you made the decision to go to medical school? After you made the decision? Or never? Maybe you simply knew in your gut what you wanted but never went through this exercise of identifying the values behind the feeling.

True clarity of your values often comes at a crisis point when you feel like you can't bear the burden of the decision one second longer. When you're exhausted from not having slept properly for days and want to quit. When you're panicked over the amount of money you owe and want to cut your losses and bail. When you've failed a test and can't bring yourself to crack open a certain book again. It's in moments like these when you ask yourself if your sacrifices are worth it. It's in moments like these that your true values become crystal clear. You look deep in your soul and find your answer. If you stay the course, then you continue on with even greater conviction. Lingering doubts fade, and you are left knowing exactly what you want for yourself.

Having your convictions tested like this can be scary, but it can also be reassuring—after the test has been passed, that is. But why wait for challenging circumstances to arise before you explore your values in depth? Why not think ahead in a proactive manner about how to build a life and career that reflects your values? I urge you not to wait until you're facing some unforeseen pressure to figure it all out. Instead, I urge you to clarify your values now, to arm yourself with the knowledge of what you stand for and why, to root yourself in the certainty of your position, and then proceed to build your career on firm moral ground.

Knowing your values as a physician and building a career in alignment with them is the best way to lead a life that feels meaningful, sustainable, and internally coherent. The alternative leads to disillusionment and disenchantment. This, unfortunately, is the underlying reason many physicians leave the profession. They feel like their values have been undermined.

Values such as:

- **Shared Dignity:** Every human being has worth and should be treated equally, regardless of physical condition or economic status.
- **Solidarity:** The doctor-patient relationship is the sacred cornerstone of medicine and is never to be violated.
- **Autonomy:** Both patient autonomy and physician autonomy should be respected.
- **Informed Consent:** Patients should be informed of all options and risks.
- **Stewardship:** Physicians must use their time, resources, and skills responsibly and wisely, protecting their patients and themselves.
- **Common Good:** Decisions (clinical and financial) should not benefit a few but rather should be win-win solutions for all.

Stripped of their values, many doctors no longer recognize themselves. This feeling of defeat builds and builds over time to the point they no longer have the heart to put in another day's work. This is a tragic outcome, especially after a person has sacrificed so much for the profession.

Part 2: When the System Has Different Values

How does something like that happen? How do doctors allow their values to be undermined? Why don't they simply speak up and say something?

Well, remember how I said earlier that changes in the system have been sneaking up on doctors in obscure ways? It's not as if someone came in with a gun and said to these physicians, "Hand over all your values or I'll shoot." No, that would have been too obvious. Instead, it happened over time, little by little, drawing minimal attention, with the changes within the system being cloaked in confusing language — language designed to convince doctors (and patients) that everyone shares the same values . . . when they don't.

Value-Based Care has become one of the most heavily marketed concepts in modern health care.

That sounds great, you think. Everyone wants healthcare based on values, right? By Value-Based Care, they must certainly mean:

- High quality care
- Efficient care
- Patient-centered care

Right?

Wrong. This goes back to what I said earlier. It's easy for highly idealistic people to assume everyone shares their values. If only that were true. So, as good as those rose-colored glasses look on you, I'm asking you to take a moment and notice that not everyone is wearing the same.

When it comes to providing healthcare, doctors define value differently from insurers and regulators. For us (and the patients, too, for that matter), value is rooted in the doctor-patient relationship and the shared decision-making that results in the best medical outcome.

Anything that weakens that relationship erodes the value of care. That seems fairly obvious. At least it does to us.

But let me tell you how insurers and regulators define value. Insurers value cost-containment. So, when it comes to treating your patient, the insurance company will endorse the least expensive treatment plan over the most effective treatment plan. Regulators value measurable compliance using standardized metrics. So, when it comes to treating your patient, regulators will demand that you engage in bureaucracy for bureaucracy's sake, regardless of its relevance and inconvenience to you and the patient.

Do you see how quickly something as innocent sounding as Value-Based Care gets muddled when we introduce the interests of two additional parties within the healthcare system?

The question now becomes whose values will prevail. At the moment, doctors are the underdogs. By controlling the narrative — and the metrics — the third-party interests (insurers and regulators) have been able to shift the focus away from individualized patient care and toward administrative checkboxes, spreadsheets, and financial targets that serve their interests first. Using benign language like Value-Based Care, they've lowered doctors' defenses and secured our compliance.

The third-party interests package their messages in slogans using persuasive language. In the hustle of daily medical practice, it's difficult for physicians to pause, dissect, and question what's actually behind the language. This is how various third-party interests take advantage of physicians' busy schedules and our collective silence to redefine care in ways that undermine our practice of medicine. It's been a slow leak, not a tidal wave. Little phrases like this become the background hum of office language and chip away at what medicine used to stand for. Bit by bit, they've hollowed out the words that once meant care, connection, and trust.

This assault on jargon is one of many reasons you must hone your critical thinking skills. Words are being used like Trojan horses to invade our mental landscape unnoticed.

Here are some other examples of how values get twisted through semantics:

System vs. Practice

Systems are great for machines, not for people. Practices, on the other hand, are built for humans. They allow space for judgment, intuition, and discretion. After all, a practice is a craft, not a cog. Do you want to be part of a system or a practice? It will depend upon your values.

Access vs. Relationship

Politicians love to promise access to care. It's their favorite word because it sounds charitable and requires no follow-up. But access without relationship is just another door to knock on. Access is a checkbox; relationship is an experience.

Health Insurance vs. Healthcare

Let's clear this one up once and for all: health insurance is not healthcare. Insurance is a toll — it decides if you're allowed to get on the highway. Healthcare is the drive itself — it is the doctor who knows you, the time spent together, the plan built for you.

Then, there are subtle shifts in language that can feel innocuous at first, but are really redefining things — including you!

Provider vs. Physician

"What do I care if the bureaucratic language refers to me as a provider?" you might ask, thinking being referred to as a *provider* doesn't diminish your distinction as a doctor in any way. Stop right there! This is exactly how physicians get marginalized within the system.

Being referred to as a *provider* manages to erase everything that makes our profession unique. It takes all our years of study, countless sleepless nights, and our solemn oath, then steamrolls them flat into a buzzword that means absolutely nothing outside billing codes. There's no such thing as Provider School. I've never heard of anyone cramming for provider board exams, have you?

Many physicians have been dismayed by the erosion of the quality of care available to patients but nonetheless have resigned themselves to the "new normal" in healthcare. They might argue they had no choice. They were caught unprepared. They assumed everyone shared the same values, and once they realized that wasn't true, well then, it was too late for them to do anything about it.

See where I am going with this?

It comes down to being prepared — to clearly identifying your values from the outset so you can recognize when they are being eroded — or worse, trampled upon.

This is why I am urging you to consciously identify your values now and to consider how you want to safeguard them in your practice. If you aren't proactive in this regard, you risk being lulled into a sense of complacency and submission through slick marketing campaigns and wolf-in-sheep's-clothing language.

It is no secret that our healthcare system feels broken from all sides. Many physicians will tell you they are overwhelmed by endless bureaucracy, unrealistic demands, and a grinding pace that can drain their passion and cloud their sense of purpose. At the same time, those receiving care often face frustration, delays, and a system that can feel impersonal and inaccessible. This disconnect leaves both caregivers and patients trapped in cycles of dissatisfaction and burnout, often feeling like there's no clear way out. Yet, the truth is that autonomy and choice — both at an individual and systemic level — can offer paths to reclaim control and reshape our experience.

As a physician you will have to decide how to reconcile these pressures with your calling to care for your patients. You might bend your practice model toward these imposed frameworks or you might chart a different path — direct primary or specialty care, concierge medicine, locums, or hybrid approaches that preserve space for authentic doctor-patient decision-making.

The good news is this: YOU have options!

And that's what this book is about: OPTIONS.

I'm so excited to help you see all the options you have ahead and to help you choose in accordance with your best interests. But remember, options come with tradeoffs. And tradeoffs are easier to accept when you have clearly identified your values. So, please don't skip that step.

Now, let me leave you with a thought that came to me recently while attending my 40th high school reunion. It's funny how these things sneak up on you — and yet, they bring a flood of memories that only get richer with time. Amid the conversations about successes and failures, beginnings and endings, what really stood out was how the perspectives we formed early in life have continued to influence us profoundly—for many, they have given us the strength to break free and choose to live intentionally in alignment with our principles.

When we were in high school, we were convinced we knew everything and certain nobody else understood the world—or our place in it. The teen angst, the restlessness, and hope of those years—it was all so vivid, even if we didn't realize how formative those moments would become.

Somewhere in the background of those years, echoing through gym dances and playing on our cassette tapes, were the lyrics of Simple Minds demanding, *Don't you forget about me!* These lyrics still ring true because all these years later, those memories—and those people—matter more than we ever imagined.

At this gathering, the conversations shifted—no longer centered on ourselves, but focused on our kids, our parents, and what lies ahead. The overall sentiment was shaped by a quiet gratitude and an openness to vulnerability, as our stories of hopes and worries about the future were shared more freely than before. There was a real sense of reflection, of appreciating both where life has led each of us and what changes and challenges still await.

What struck me was how, no matter where life had taken everyone—different cities, different paths—there's something genuine, common, and unchanged about the perspectives we carry. Those early years clearly planted deep roots. While the people we've become have been shaped by so many things, the foundations that were created in those formative years—full of insecurity, passion, searching, and unforgettable anthems of resilience—still hold a powerful influence.

It's a reminder that the choices we make early on can impact far more than you can ever imagine in the moment. Life's messy and complicated, and nowhere is that more evident than in healthcare, where chaos and constant change test our resilience and purpose. Yet, that is exactly where autonomy comes in—the freedom to choose how you live, how you practice, and who you want to be amid the demands.

So, you see, the ball's in your court.

It's your move.

Let's go.

CHAPTER TWO

MONEY 101

Making Your First Paychecks Count

Have you ever heard the phrase, "Health is wealth?" I love that phrase. It sums up, in three little words, a basic truth that so many people overlook in their lives. Without health, material wealth doesn't matter much.

In your medical practice, however, your financial health is what keeps everything else alive. Without financial health, nothing else works for long. Your practice folds. Your patients receive no care. Your years of hard work fall flat.

So, just as I want my patients to prioritize their health, I want you, in your medical career (however it might look, wherever it might take you), to prioritize financial health.

You'd be surprised at how many doctors avoid taking a close look at the financial workings of their life and their practice. It's not their comfort zone, I guess. They prefer to remain in their own domain and outsource the financial component to a "trusted" source. However, remember the age-old adage: Trust but verify.

I'm all in favor of delegating work within my practice, but at the end of the day, the buck always stops with me. I must verify that all work performed in my practice meets my standards, and that includes the financial work. So even if you don't manage the books or arrange the financing yourself, you do need to verify that what is done is being done properly. And that means you'll have to dig in a little and get yourself up to speed on the financial operations of your practice. This applies regardless of the type of practice you pursue.

In this chapter, I'm not trying to turn you into a financial planner. I want to give you just enough clarity and confidence around money so that it supports your career choices instead of boxing you in.

Getting Started

There is no better time to start building strong financial acumen than the moment you decide to matriculate toward a medical degree. No worries if you haven't considered it until now; now is better than later. Your financial profile will be relatively straightforward compared to where it will likely be years and decades from now. The goal should be to develop rock-solid healthy habits around money when the tasks are less daunting, so that these habits remain firmly in place over the years as your financial circumstances become more complex—as you buy property, invest in a practice, hire employees, etc. Trust me, the healthy habits you build right out of medical school will pay off in spades as you grow professionally.

Let's start with something really basic: managing your paycheck as a resident.

You will soon receive your first employment and compensation package. For many, this will be the first time you deal with compensation details this complex. Spoiler alert: It only grows more complicated with each passing year.

A paycheck doesn't automatically provide peace of mind. Peace of mind comes from planning and maybe even unlearning some old habits. Money is more than simply math. Money is emotional. It brings up feelings of stress, scarcity, maybe a pressure to "catch up," or even a burst of rebellion (I deserve this vacation after all those nights on call!). If anything, money can rob you of peace of mind.

Or maybe you think money is boring. A term like cash flow brings on a yawn. It sounds like a simple concept. And indeed, the concept is easy: how much money is coming in and where it is going. But in practice, cash flow is not always as easy as it sounds—especially when, for the first time ever, you actually have options.

After you've spent years surviving on crumbs, receiving a multi-figure package might leave you feeling giddy and light-headed. You might even feel quite flush—so much so that when it comes to making purchases, money will seem like no object. It's a common phenomenon among students graduating from medical school. The long-awaited promise day arrives, and now they're rich! Money troubles are over. Let the spending begin.

Not so fast.

If you have been living without money, you have not had to make many decisions about spending money. The decisions were made for you. You survived on peanut butter sandwiches and coffee and whatever you could get for free from the hospital. You wore scrubs every day. You took the bus or walked. You entertained yourself by staring at the sunset. Nothing wrong with any of that. The best part of not having any money is not having to think about money.

To be honest, for all the years spent memorizing metabolic pathways and rare diseases, most highly educated physicians leave training with a six-figure salary and a six-year-old's understanding of personal finance. If that's you, you're not behind—you're just untrained in a subject no one bothered to teach you.

There's this weird moment no one really prepares you for: Your first real doctor paycheck lands in your bank account. The first feeling is relief. The next is pride. And then comes panic.

I call this the "Where Did My Paycheck Go?" principle. Here's your first lesson: Your gross salary is NOT your takehome pay. The gross pay number might look shockingly large—until you realize how many little nibbles are being taken out of it. Taxes, retirement contributions, insurance premiums, loan payments, and a few mystery deductions will take a bite out of every check. The number on your contract is just the starting point.

What matters is what actually lands in your bank account—and what you do with it next. Because there's rent, there's the car you promised yourself you'd upgrade to, and there's the weird guilt of buying brand-name cereal.

The Elephant in the Room: Student Loans

And then for many, there's the biggest elephant in the room: student loans. You, like most medical students, have probably taken on debt to finance your degree. Because you are still in school, you have enjoyed a reprieve from having to think about that debt. Out of sight, out of mind, for many. Totally understandable since you have plenty of other things vying for your attention. But before long, repayment of those loans will become a reality you will have no choice but to think about.

I'll say it for you now: **Student loans are emotionally and financially heavy.** You don't need to dive into every repayment plan and acronym today, but you do need to acknowledge the existence of your loans. No hiding under the covers.

Your loan amount might be wildly different from that of your colleagues, and your repayment options might be too. This is one area that needs a personal plan, not a generic one-size-fits-all strategy. Talk to your servicer. Ask questions. If it feels overwhelming (and it probably will), get help from someone who knows what they're doing. You're not expected to solve it all alone.

After graduating from medical school and starting your residency, you will have two choices. You can either start repaying your loans, or you can postpone repayment during residency with a mandatory medical residency forbearance. Most medical students defer repayment during the course of their training. This can be a good thing... and a bad thing.

It's good because you will be living on a tight budget as it is during those years. Not having to make loan payments will come as a relief. So, how is it a bad thing, then? Well, your total amount of debt will grow during those years as your interest gets added to the loan balance. Three to five years of full forbearance can add a painful amount to what you ultimately owe. It can be quite a shock when you finally take a look at the balance due and see how much it has risen.

As a resident, your income most likely won't support the standard ten-year repayment schedule of your loans. So, if you do decide to start loan repayment while in training, there are income-driven repayment (IDR) plans that will adjust your monthly payment to align with your ability to repay based on income. IDR plans can make student loan repayment during residency feasible and may also keep the clock moving for certain forgiveness programs.

No matter what you decide to do during your training years, every graduating medical student should understand their loans as clearly as they understand a patient's chart. There is no excuse for looking the other way. You have the brainpower; you just need the willpower — and maybe the humility to ask for help in an area where you are not an expert. While in residency, keep these simple goals in mind:

- Remain in good standing on all loans.
- Keep your payments (if you choose to start repayment) manageable according to your income.
- Position yourself for loan forgiveness and/or future aggressive payoff.

Thinking about your student loans doesn't always have to bring tears to your eyes. I recently came across the online posts by Dr. Brandon Axelrod, a surgical resident in New York City with over $400,000 in student loans who came up with a fun and creative way to bring in a little extra cash. He monetizes videos of himself performing magic and creating elaborate balloon art—two skills he honed for years as an in-person performer at events. He can actually fashion balloons into a giant lidocaine needle.

This creative young resident commented in the article about the various misperceptions people have about residents. "The resident role gets lost in the shuffle," he says. "I'm seen either as a student or as a millionaire." He has had people criticize him for monetizing his TikTok posts because they assume he's making a big paycheck and shouldn't be looking for more money.

You, too, might have people in your life assume your financial circumstances have drastically improved simply because you've completed medical school. Don't be surprised if you have to set them straight. Certainly don't try to keep up with their misperception of your financial reality. And if you have an easy, fun side gig that brings in a little extra money without interfering with your busy schedule, by all means, pursue it and pay that debt down even faster.

Building Healthy Habits Takes Work

There are volumes of books available for you to read on this subject, and countless influencers to follow online. So, I won't go into too much detail here about the art of building strong habits in general. I would simply say this: A habit is a routine behavior, and building a habit requires intentional repetition of that behavior. Bad habits do not make you a bad person. They just mean you have work to do to change the behavior. It's all about behavior modification, and there are many strategies for that. It's not all about white-knuckling it.

To keep things simple, let's focus on three basic money habits you should build early:

- Tracking your money
- Building your savings
- Surrounding yourself with trusted advisors

Tracking Your Money

These days remote sensors and fitness trackers are all the rage. Health fanatics track their sleep down to the minute, their movement down to the step, their glucose levels down to the mg/ml. Maybe you are one who is fascinated with monitoring your biorhythms and tweaking your behavior to achieve better and better results.

Either way, can you imagine getting just as excited about tracking your money as biohackers do about tracking their biodata? Imagine feeling gleeful when you manage to spend less than budgeted one week, and the surplus automatically increases the balance in your savings account or reduces the balance on your loans.

To build a habit of tracking money, apply the same basic habit principles:

- **Be specific rather than vague.** Rather than sporadically taking a look at your finances, make a concrete plan. Dedicate a particular time and place to routinely sit down and look at what's going on with your money. It could be that you decide to do this every Sunday from four to five in the afternoon. Just one hour, one day per week. Give yourself credit for showing up and keeping the commitment to yourself. Before long, this will feel comfortable and familiar. You might even look forward to this time.

- **Line up your desired behavior with the path of least resistance.** What might a path of least resistance look like when it comes to tracking your money? Money apps are probably the most resistance-free way. Of course, there is an upfront investment of time to get started. To remove your resistance to setting up the app to begin with, you could buddy up with someone else who shares the same goal and can ease the burden by joining you in the task.
- **Use positive language around the behavior.** Tracking your money can feel like a chore. But being aware of where your money is going is empowering. Be sure your language reflects that sense of empowerment.

Budgeting and tracking your spending don't have to make you miserable. The goal isn't to eliminate all joy from your life; it's to make sure you know where your money is going so you can keep more of it for what matters. Think of your budget as a Money Map—a simple, visual way to track income, expenses, savings, and debt payments. Start by listing your fixed costs (housing, loans, insurance, groceries, transportation), then estimate your discretionary spending (eating out, entertainment, travel), and see what's left for savings or debt payoff.

You've probably heard that skipping your daily coffee will make you a millionaire. The truth? It's not the $5 latte that's keeping you from financial freedom; it's the big-ticket items: housing, cars, and lifestyle creep. Focus on keeping the major expenses under control and let yourself enjoy small pleasures guilt-free.

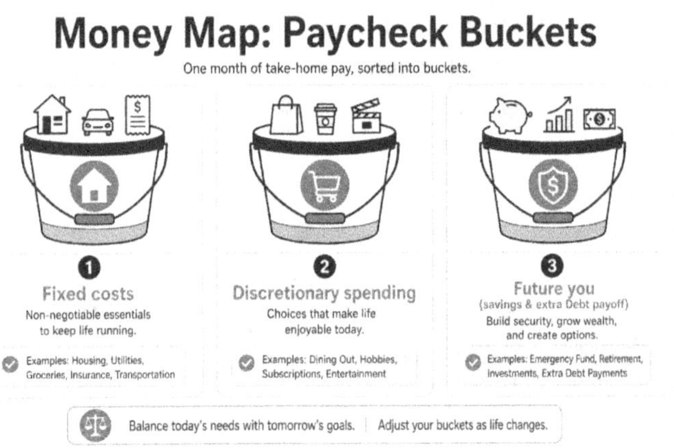

Figure 1: *Your Money Map is just a snapshot of where your paycheck actually goes. Seeing your income poured into fixed costs, discretionary spending, and savings or debt payoff on one page makes it easier to ask, "Does this match what I say I value?" You don't have to get it perfect—you just need to see the buckets clearly enough to start shifting them on purpose.*

When that first real paycheck hits, you'll want to think about the following:

- Rent or mortgage
- Loan minimums (yes, even the ones deferred and you're ignoring for now)
- Saving for emergencies (3–6 months of expenses, eventually)

- Investing for later
- Treating yourself responsibly

You don't have to get everything right immediately. You just have to start paying attention. Baby steps in the right direction will lead to strong habits over time.

If You Have a Partner

If you're in a relationship or marriage, these conversations matter even more.

Combining finances—either fully or partially—means talking about priorities, debt, spending habits, and goals. It's not always easy, especially when one of you (or both) has student loans lurking in the background like financial ghosts.

Start small. "What are we trying to accomplish this year with our money?" is a much better question than "Why did you spend $82 on bath bombs?"

And remember—your financial goals don't have to match your partner's exactly, but they do have to respect and support each other.

Build Up Your Savings

Nothing new here. Everyone should start building their savings as soon as possible. Even small, automatic transfers into a basic savings account count. An emergency fund is not a luxury; it's what keeps a flat tire, a broken appliance, or a family crisis from pushing you straight into high-interest debt.

Find Your Trusted Advisors

No one expects you to figure everything out alone. Financial decisions are complicated and have long-lasting impacts. Even if everyone around you is nodding like they've figured it all out—odds are, they probably haven't.

It's never too early to start building a strong team of advisors around you. You will need:

- A good accountant (especially if you moonlight or have side income)
- A fee-only financial advisor
- A lawyer

And yes, it is 100% OK to ask your family for advice (even your parents)—if they're financially literate and open to helping.

If someone's "advice" is mostly about selling you a product, pause and get a second opinion. And remember, never let pride keep you from asking questions. Asking questions isn't a weakness. It's initiative.

Key Takeaway

Money shouldn't be a source of shame or stress. With a few practical tools and the right mindset, you can take control of your finances—no matter where you're starting from. You've done the hard work to become a doctor. Now it's time to make sure your money habits support the kind of life and practice you actually want.

CHAPTER THREE

INSURANCE & RISK

Protecting Your Life, License, and Livelihood

Let's be honest: Insurance is not the most thrilling topic. Most new doctors would rather review a stack of consult notes than decode disability policies or malpractice coverage. But here's the truth: Insurance is your real-world PPE. You hope you never need it, but if you ever do, you'll be very glad it's there.

Insurance is not glamorous, but it's crucial—and no one hands you a decoder ring for it. You're in a profession where one unexpected event or one tiny clause in your policy (or omitted from your policy) can change everything. This isn't to scare you. It's to encourage you to stop blindly clicking through insurance forms like they're software updates.

In this chapter, I am not going to cover every possible policy. I am going to focus on the core coverage you actually need as a physician, so you can protect yourself without getting lost in the weeds.

Why Insurance Feels So Confusing

Because it **IS** confusing. And what's more frustrating: It is complicated by design. The amount of jargon, acronyms, riders, exclusions, and paperwork can feel endless. By comparison, insurance contracts can make your EMR look simple. No one really tells you what you actually need: what kind of coverage and how much.

Here are some questions you might be asking yourself:

- Do I need life insurance if I'm single?
- Is disability insurance just for thrill-seekers?
- Doesn't the hospital handle malpractice?
- What's an own-occupation policy?
- Is umbrella insurance real, or just a Mary Poppins thing?

Let's tackle the basics—no fluff, no scare tactics.

The Big Three You Need to Know

Disability Insurance (aka The Ultimate Safety Net)

If you lose the ability to work—temporarily or permanently—this is the insurance that replaces your income. But be careful: Not all policies are created equal.

Here's what you want to ask for: an **own-occupation** policy that protects you if you can't perform your specific specialty. Language matters here. You want to be protected if you cannot do the job you were trained for—not told to go find some other job. Can you imagine being told by an insurance company to take a job as a phone rep after you've trained twelve years to perform surgery? No thanks.

When should you look into getting disability insurance? Yesterday. Or today, if you are healthy. Rates are lowest when you are young and a good risk. Even while you are in training, many companies offer resident-friendly starter policies with options to increase the coverage in years ahead.

Life Insurance (aka Planning for "What If")

No one in their 20s or 30s loves thinking about life insurance. But if there's anyone who depends on your income (a spouse, kids, aging parents, even a shared mortgage holder), it's time to put life insurance on your radar.

At its core, life insurance is about protecting those who rely on you financially if something unexpected happens. It's not about betting on doom. It's about giving your family breathing room in the event of the worst-case scenario.

There are two major categories you'll hear about:

- **Term Life Insurance** covers you for a specific period of time (such as ten, twenty, or thirty years). It's typically less expensive and is often used to cover things like debts, mortgages, or income replacement during your peak earning years.

- **Permanent Life Insurance** (such as whole life, universal life, variable life) lasts your entire life, often comes with a savings or investment component, and is more expensive.

Some people use life insurance for estate planning or other long-term financial strategies. This is something you might want to ask your agent or financial advisor about once your overall plan is clearer.

Each type has pros, cons, and lots of subflavors. The "right" choice depends on your goals, your family situation, your debts, and your broader financial plan.

Here's the most important thing: *Talk to someone who knows this stuff well.*

A good life insurance broker can walk you through the differences and help you compare actual quotes from different companies. A fee-only financial advisor can help you understand how life insurance fits into your bigger financial picture.

Just remember—life insurance isn't a one-size-fits-all proposition. There's no shame in saying, "Can you explain this again like I'm five?" That's what experts are for.

Malpractice Insurance (aka Please Don't Sue Me Insurance)

If you're employed by a hospital or large group, chances are your malpractice insurance is already taken care of. But don't assume you're covered for every eventually. Take a closer look.

There are two main types of malpractice policies: **claims-made** and **occurrence.** The first thing you need to do is check which type your employer has provided for you.

- A **claims-made policy** will protect you if the policy is active both when (1) the incident happens and (2) when a claim is filed. If you leave your job or switch insurers, you'll need to buy **tail coverage** to remain protected from claims that could pop up later.
- An **occurrence policy** covers you for anything that happened while the policy was active, even if a claim comes years down the line—no extra tail coverage needed.

Tail coverage extends malpractice protection for a fixed period of time, even if you cancel the coverage yourself. For example, imagine you have malpractice coverage in place from 2000–2005 with Company A and then switch to a different plan with Company B in 2006. Now imagine it is 2012 and someone files a claim on damages that occurred in 2003 and names you in the filing. With tail coverage, this claim will be covered by Company A, even if you have not been paying premiums to that company since 2005. You will pay additional premiums for tail coverage, but it is well worth it in these instances.

Most malpractice tail endorsements are offered in set terms (e.g., 1, 2, 3, 5 years) or as unlimited/lifetime tails. Many carriers default to or strongly recommend an unlimited tail because claims can arise well beyond standard statutes of limitation, especially with discovery-rule extensions and for pediatric, obstetric, or delayed-diagnosis cases. In many states, especially if you treat children, a claim can be filed by an adult who received care from you when they were a minor.

Also, don't forget to ask your carrier about potential gaps in coverage. Moonlighting, telemedicine, and side gigs are not always included under your main policy. If you're doing any work outside your primary job, make sure it's covered under your malpractice policy—or consider getting a separate policy to cover your side work.

Bottom line:

- Ask questions.
- Know what's covered.
- Don't assume one policy fits all.

A little homework now can save you a lot of stress (and money) if you ever find yourself facing a lawsuit.

A Few Honorable Mentions

- **Renter's/Homeowner's Insurance:** If you have stuff and you care about it, insure it.
- **Umbrella Insurance:** A personal liability add-on that isn't too expensive could be helpful once your net worth begins to grow. Think of it as extra padding on your homeowner's/renter's/auto policies.

And Finally, Health Insurance

Navigating health insurance can feel like trying to read a map in a foreign language. As a young physician, you've probably heard that you need coverage to protect yourself from those "just in case" moments. And yes, health insurance is a smart way to manage risk in your personal life, so you're not blindsided by unexpected medical bills.

But here's the twist: **Health insurance doesn't actually**

get you care—it is a means to pay for it but keep in mind, it's not the only way to pay for services.

As a patient, it's easy to think, I need insurance or else I can't see a doctor. But as a physician, you have the ability to provide care to your patient whether they have insurance or not. This is an important distinction, and it can help you avoid falling into the trap of thinking insurance is always the only answer.

Now, if your employer is offering you health insurance as part of your benefits package, chances are you'll take it—and that's usually a good move. Employer-sponsored plans often come with lower premiums and broader coverage than what you'd find on your own. But don't just sign up and forget about it. Take a little time to actually look at what's included.

- What's your deductible?
- Which doctors are in-network?
- Are there exclusions or hoops you have to jump through for certain treatments?

Understanding your plan now can save you headaches (and money) down the road.

Remember, there are other financial vehicles beyond traditional health insurance to help manage healthcare expenses and reduce out-of-pocket costs for individuals, such as:

- Health savings accounts (HSA)
- Flexible savings accounts (FSA)
- Health reimbursement arrangements (HRAs)

- Supplemental insurance policies

Just ask your broker or benefits representative about the options available.

How to Shop for Insurance Without Being Sold

Every successful physician has a behind-the-scenes trio making sure their foundation and coverage are solid:

- A trustworthy **accountant** who understands physician finances, can help you maximize deductions, and keeps you out of tax trouble.
- A reliable **attorney** who will review contracts, explain legalese, and advocate for your interests when you need it most.
- An **insurance broker** who is your advocate—not just a salesperson. This person should explain your options to you in plain language, compare policies across companies, and help you find the right fit for your unique needs.

When you start looking for "a good insurance person," it helps to know they don't all do the same job. One camp deals with **property and casualty**—think auto, home, and business liability—while another focuses on **health and life**, like disability, health insurance, and life coverage for you, your family, or your practice. You want the right kind of agent for the right kind of problem, so don't be afraid to ask, "What do you specialize in—and what don't you do?" and, when possible, build a small bench of trusted people instead of expecting one agent to cover everything.

Look for an **independent insurance broker** who works with multiple companies and is focused on finding the best fit for you—not just selling a particular product. A good broker will take the time to explain your choices, answer your questions, and help you navigate changes as your needs evolve. Not all brokers are created equal, so seek out someone who listens, advocates for you, and offers ongoing service—not just a quick sale.

Don't automatically settle for the insurance broker your employer recommends. Talk with them first. Ask your colleagues for referrals. If a broker doesn't leave you feeling clearer, smarter, and more secure after your conversation, keep looking. Your future self will thank you.

Final Thoughts

You don't need to be paranoid—you just need to be prepared. Insurance isn't glamorous, but it's a way of saying, "I care about protecting the life I'm working so hard to build." Insurance isn't about expecting the worst. It's about making sure one bad day doesn't become a disaster.

You don't have to know everything. You just have to know enough to ask good questions, protect your future self, and surround yourself with a team you trust. Take a breath. You've got this. And remember, the right insurance coverage doesn't mean fear—it means freedom.

SECTION ONE WRAP-UP

DOCTOR DO ✔

- ☑ **Do know what you stand for.** Name your core personal and professional values—on paper, not just in your head. Use your actual choices so far (including choosing medicine) as evidence of what you truly care about, not what you think you "should" value.

- ☑ **Do notice misalignment early.** Pay attention when something feels "off"—a job description, a productivity expectation, a policy that clashes with how you believe medicine should be practiced. That discomfort is data, not a personal failing.

- ☑ **Do learn the basics of your money.** Understand the difference between your gross salary and what actually hits your bank account. Know your student loan totals and your current repayment or forbearance status. Start tracking where your money goes, even if it's messy at first.

- ☑ **Do treat your financial habits as part of patient care.** Healthy money habits—budgeting, living below your means, building savings—aren't just about wealth. They're what keep you from being forced into jobs, schedules, and contracts that grind down your values.

- ☑ **Do protect your life, license, and livelihood.** Make sure you have the core coverage appropriate to your stage: own occupation disability insurance, appropriate life insurance if someone depends on your income, and malpractice coverage you actually understand (including whether you need tail).

- ☑ **Do build a small, trusted team.** Seek out an accountant, attorney, and insurance broker who can explain things in plain language and who are clearly on your side. Ask what they specialize in, what they don't do, and how they're compensated.

DOCTOR DON'T ✖

- **Don't assume everyone shares your values.** Just because a policy or program uses words like "value," "quality," or "patient-centered" doesn't mean it honors the doctor-patient relationship the way you do.

- **Don't wait for a crisis to find out what matters.** Burnout, moral injury, financial panic, or a lawsuit are miserable times to discover you've been out of alignment for years. Do the values work before you're under fire.

- **Don't confuse a big salary with financial security.** The number on your contract is not your real spending power. Lifestyle creep, debt, and a lack of planning can make a six -figure income feel just as stressful as your student days.

- **Don't ignore your loans or "hope they work out."** Silence and avoidance are not strategies. You don't have to have every answer today, but you do need to know your totals, your terms, and your options.

- **Don't blindly trust that you're covered.** Never assume "the hospital handles that" or "HR already took care of it" when it comes to malpractice, disability, or health coverage. If you haven't seen it and don't understand it, you don't really know what you have.

- **Don't settle for the first advisor or broker who crosses your path.** If a conversation leaves you feeling confused, pressured, or talked down to, that is your sign to keep looking. The right advisors make you feel clearer and more confident, not smaller.

WHY IT MATTERS

Values, money, and insurance may not feel as exciting as diagnoses and procedures, but they quietly determine what kind of doctor you get to be—and for how long. When your values are clear, your finances are stable, and your risks are reasonably covered, you make decisions from a place of strength instead of fear. You're much less likely to wake up ten years from now wondering how you ended up in a version of medicine that doesn't feel like yours.

Getting your house in order now doesn't make you selfish or "too focused on the business side." It makes you a better steward of your calling, your patients, and the life you've worked so hard to build.

PUTTING IT INTO PRACTICE

You don't have to fix everything at once. Start with a few concrete steps:

Write your non-negotiables. Take ten to fifteen minutes to list your top five to seven values as a physician and as a person (for example: clinical excellence, time with patients, family, faith, autonomy, financial stability). Next to each, jot down one real decision you've already made that reflects that value.

Do a "first paycheck" reality check. Take a sample resident or attending pay stub (or an online calculator) and walk through it line by line. Note your gross pay, taxes, benefits, and what your true take-home would be. Then list your major expenses (housing, loans, essentials) to see what's left.

Face your loans on paper. Write down your total student loan balance, interest rates, servicers, and current status (in school, grace, forbearance, or repayment). You don't have to choose a long-term strategy yet. Just know your numbers.

List your current and needed coverage. On one page, list what you have now: health, malpractice, disability, life, renter's/homeowner's, any others. Next to that, mark what you *think* you need but don't have yet. Circle one to learn more about this month.

Pick one of these to do this week. Put it on your calendar like any other important appointment. This is part of taking care of your first patient — YOU — so that you can keep taking care of everyone else.

SECTION TWO

HOW THE SYSTEM ACTUALLY WORKS

CHAPTER FOUR

EMPLOYMENT MODELS

Know What You're Signing Up For

Imagine this scenario: Your training is behind you, and the world of medicine is wide open and finally yours to shape and make of it what you have always dreamed of. Maybe you're just starting to contemplate your next move. Or perhaps you're already looking through a stack of offer letters. Either way, there's a big fork in the road ahead. This fork is a juncture in a physician's career that, for some reason, rarely gets the attention it deserves but yet will impact everything that comes after it.

You basically have two choices at this point. You can work for someone else. Or you can take a leap of faith and work for yourself. The choice is all yours.

Either way, there is something you need to take a moment and wrap your head around first. For many years now, you've been pursuing your dream of becoming a doctor within a system designed to help you succeed and move forward. I'm not saying your education and training hasn't been strenuous. Of course, it has. And, indeed, some people haven't made it through. But the system itself is designed to support your success. Medical schools don't want to see anyone drop out, and they shouldn't. You are paying them a hefty sum to educate you. That's their job.

However, once you cross the threshold, leave the world of academics and training behind, and begin your medical practice, the financial equation reverses. You are no longer the payor, entitled to receive something. You become the payee. Medical schools and residencies owe you an education and training. But once you graduate, no one owes you anything. Of course, employers owe you payment for your services, but they don't owe you any certain amount. Everything at that point–from salary to bonus to case load to hours worked–will be negotiable. And the art of negotiation is not something taught in medical school.

What is deemed fair payment and/or fair working arrangements will be up for debate. Those paying will have their definition. You will have your own. So, what do you do about that? Well, you learn the system. You learn how it works and how to make it work for you. Trust me. If you don't do that, the system will be more than happy to make YOU work for IT.

Wait, What Am I... W2 or 1099?

Let's start with something basic: the employment models available to physicians. At the end of the day (April 15th, that is), you'll either file as a W2 employee or a 1099 independent contractor... or maybe both. However, before you sign that first contract or start designing your own clinic logo in your mind, you need to understand what forms of employment you are choosing between. It's worth taking a step back and getting familiar with the ways in which physicians actually work today. What each option entails. What they both look like.

These days, you have multiple options, each with its own mix of perks, trade-offs, and realities that aren't always spelled out for you in the job description. Whether you crave the security of a big hospital system or the independence of running your own shop—or something in between—understanding these employment models is the first step in building a career that actually fits your life and matches your values.

Let's break down the typical paths you'll see as you launch into practice.

Option One: Employment (aka Team Hospital or Mega Group)

This is the most common route these days for graduating physicians–and for good reason. It's immediate. It's straightforward. It requires little additional work on your part. It's the path most of your peers will follow. You finish residency or fellowship, sign a contract, and the paychecks start showing up. Let's call this the path of least resistance. Now let's break down what you get and what you give up: the tradeoff calculation.

What you get:

- A steady paycheck (plus bonus in some cases)
- Malpractice coverage

- A benefits package you don't have to negotiate
- Administrative support: billing, scheduling, HR, coding
- Predictable schedule (usually)
- A built-in referral network

What you give up:

- Control over your schedule
- Control over how the clinic is run
- The ability to negotiate your compensation after you sign
- The ability to experiment with new ways of delivering services (i.e. cash-pay services or telehealth)

In theory, working for an employer allows you to focus all your attention on your patients, clock out at the end of the day, and leave the headaches at the office. There's comfort in knowing that if the EMR crashes, someone else is on call to fix it.

There are many reasons why Option One might make sense for you and be your best choice. At this point, you've been through years and years of intense coursework and training. Many people in your shoes just need some time to breathe and get comfortable with the transition to becoming a fully practicing physician without an additional learning curve. You might be feeling burned out on the books and memorization and simply want to practice medicine without having to learn things like QuickBooks and payroll management. Employment offers you a soft landing.

However, don't mistake easy onboarding for long-term alignment with your goals and values. And don't sleep on the job when it comes to advocating for yourself as each year passes.

Option Two: Independent Practice (aka Flying Solo or with a Few Trusted Friends)

On the other side, there is that lure of independence. Maybe you dream of setting your own schedule, building a practice around your unique values, or choosing which patients you see and how you care for them. The idea of autonomy is tempting. There is no one there looking over your shoulder, no productivity quotas, and no corporate memos dictating your day.

This is the model most of my generation and mentors trained under. It has drifted in and out of style. These days, it is a good bit less common than when I graduated–though not fully extinct. Actually, there are signs that private practice might be experiencing a bit of a resurgence. For the right person, independent practice can be incredibly rewarding.

What you get:

- Greater autonomy over your schedule, staffing, and clinical model
- Potential for higher long-term income
- The flexibility to build niche services, hybrid models, and concierge offerings
- The satisfaction of building something that is yours

What you give up:

- Up-front investment of funds to cover start-up costs (EMR, rent, legal services, staff, equipment.)
- Up-front investment of time to learn the business side: payroll, benefits, billing
- Financial certainty (All business ventures involve a measure of risk.)
- Pride (It takes humility to ask for help when you don't understand the business side of your practice.)

Independent practice is like opening a restaurant. Your restaurant can be amazing, but you'll work hard, especially early on. You'll wear hats you didn't know existed (hello, marketing strategy and lease negotiation). It can feel overwhelming at times—but it will also feel empowering.

Pro tip: You don't have to go it alone. You can partner with other physicians, hire coaches, and outsource services for things like billing. An experienced private practice manager will be able to help with many of the tasks. Again: Ask for help! Don't try to do this alone.

Option Three: The Hybrid Life (aka The Best of Both Worlds... or the Busiest)

Some physicians opt to start out their careers within the safety of full employment and later shift to independence. Others blend the two models. They work half the week as employees and the other half the week in a private capacity. Or they open a side hustle clinic while working as a full-time employee.

In today's evolving healthcare universe, creative models are on the rise. You find a variety of arrangements such as:

- Concierge medicine
- Direct care practices: direct primary care (DPC) or direct specialty care (DSC)
- Locum tenens
- Telehealth-only practices

Deciding which path to take goes beyond the question of freedom versus stability. It comes down to knowing yourself. Here are some of the big questions you need to ponder:

- How much risk are you willing to take on for the sake of having more control?
- How do you react to and deal with uncertainty?
- Can you manage a staff?
- Are you energized by the idea of building something from scratch, or do you prefer the predictability of a well-oiled machine?

Ask yourself the following questions:

- Do I want full control over my practice, or do I prefer to have more support right now?
- How much risk can I reasonably take on—financially and emotionally?
- Am I willing to spend time learning about business, or do I want to focus only on patient care?

- Could I try one model now and consider switching later?
- Do I know someone already doing what I want to do?

Answering these questions will require you to dig deep and explore those core values we discussed in Chapter One.

When confronted with the big fork in the road ahead, there's no universal right answer—just the right answer for you at that moment. Take a deep breath and keep in mind that, no matter what you choose, you can always change course down the road.

Your Work Environment / Pick Your Poison: Academic, Corporate, Private

So far, we've talked about how you might work: employed, independent, or hybrid. Now let's talk about *where* you might work. Although there are other settings, the most common three are academic, corporate, and private.

Academic medicine involves teaching and research and will provide you with a steady paycheck. You'll have a hand in shaping the next generation, which can be quite rewarding. You'll probably publish a paper or two. And you'll attend more committee meetings than you ever thought possible. The prestige is real, but so is the bureaucracy.

Corporate or employed positions—think big hospital systems—offer stability and a benefits package that rivals your favorite coffee shop's menu. You'll have predictable hours, a regular paycheck, and less administrative hassle. The trade-off? Less control over your schedule, patient load, and sometimes even your clinical decisions.

Private practice is for those who want autonomy and are willing to take on some risk. Maybe you dream of partnership, or even owning your own clinic someday (or maybe not—you simply don't want to be in an academic or corporate setting, and we'll come back to that in a little bit). You'll get closer to the business side of medicine, and you might have more say in how things are run. But remember, with great power comes... a lot of paperwork.

Remember, you're not just picking a model—you're picking a setting, a culture, and a set of expectations.

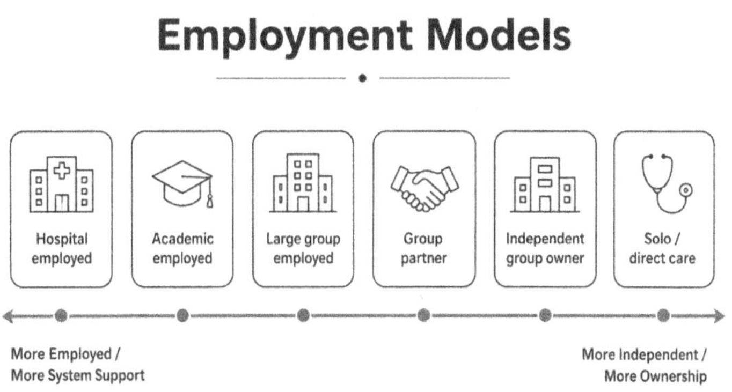

Figure 2: *This spectrum isn't about right or wrong; it's about trade-offs. On the left are models with more built-in support and stability, and on the right are models with more ownership and control—and more responsibility. As you look across the line, notice which boxes feel like your default and which ones quietly pull at you. That curiosity is worth listening to as you design the kind of career you actually want.*

Comparison Is a Rigged Game

There's a common misconception in medicine that you have to be the "top doc" to be successful or fulfilled—especially in private practice. From early training, physicians are encouraged to aim high, take charge, and ultimately lead, so it's easy to internalize the idea that anything short of ownership or leadership is somehow falling short. That mindset can quietly shape career decisions, even when it doesn't align with what actually brings satisfaction or balance. Many doctors end up chasing roles they think they should want, rather than pausing to ask what kind of day-to-day life they truly prefer.

But here's the truth: Not everyone needs—or even wants—to be the one running the show. Leadership comes with its own set of pressures that aren't always visible from the outside, and those responsibilities don't appeal to everyone. The "queen bee" model can be misleading because it suggests that value is tied to status, when in reality, fulfillment often comes from alignment with your strengths and priorities. There's no universal blueprint for what a successful medical career has to look like.

Think of a hive: Every role matters, and the entire system depends on people doing different kinds of work well. Worker bees aren't lesser—they're essential. In the same way, physicians who choose not to own or manage a practice play a critical role in delivering care, maintaining continuity, and supporting the overall health of the organization. Their contributions are no less meaningful simply because they don't carry the title of owner or partner.

You might find that you love the culture and flexibility of private practice but have zero interest in managing payroll, negotiating leases, or taking on the financial and administrative burden of ownership. In that case, choosing to be a physician employee isn't a compromise—it's a strategic decision. It can create a win-win dynamic where practice owners have reliable, dedicated clinicians, and physicians can focus their time and energy on patient care and personal well-being. You don't have to be in charge to have a meaningful, rewarding career; sometimes the best fit is being a valued part of a strong team in a setting that lets you do what you love most.

Remember, you're not just picking a job—you're picking a lifestyle, a culture, and a set of expectations. The "right" model is the one that fits you right now. And if your needs change down the road, that's not failure—that is growth.

So, as you weigh your options, remember: It's your career. Your life. Your call.

CHAPTER FIVE

MEET THE PAYORS

Follow The Money

If you want to make sense of how money moves in medicine from payor to payee, you've got to know who's actually footing the bill. You also need to know that it's not always a straight line from one to the other. Don't worry—I'll keep it simple and practical.

First Up, The Federal Players

Medicare is the big one for patients sixty-five and older (and some with disabilities). It pays according to fee schedules that are set by the government. No negotiations. You simply take it or leave it.

Tricare and the **Veterans Administration (VA)** take care of active-duty military, veterans, and their families. They have their own rules and quirks, but they're considered part of the federal mix.

Then There Are The State Players

Medicaid covers low-income patients, but there is a catch: Every state runs its own version, so what you get paid (and how easy it is to get paid) can vary widely depending on where you practice. Reimbursement is usually on the lower end. Also, no negotiations.

Some states have their own Medicaid expansions or insurance exchanges, which can add another layer of rules (and paperwork) to the mix.

And Finally, The Commercial Crowd

Think Blue Cross, United Healthcare, Cigna, Aetna, and Humana (in some circles referred to as BUCAH)—all the big names you see on insurance cards. These plans are either provided through employers or purchased directly by patients.

Here's where things get interesting (but not in a fun way): The amount each commercial insurer pays out for a service isn't set in stone. Rather, reimbursement rates are all about contracts—negotiated between the insurer and your practice or hospital. That means two clinics across the street from each other could, in practice, receive totally different rates for the same service.

Each payor shows up with its own fee schedules, pre-authorization hoops, claim review processes, and (yes) plenty of fine print.

This insurance mix affects your compensation, your practice's bottom line, and—sometimes—how much time you get to spend with each patient.

The better you understand who's paying (and how they calculate payment), the less surprised you'll be when you see how your work actually gets reimbursed.

How This Works in Reality

You might bill $300 for a visit, but the insurer only pays $90.

The rest? It will be written off, adjusted, or lost in the black hole of "denied claims."

Bonuses are often tied to collections, Relative Value Units (RVUs), or some mix of both. I go into this in greater detail in the next chapter, but for now, these are the questions you need to ask:

Is my bonus based on gross charges or net collections?

Will I be penalized for patients who can't pay or for insurance denials?

Does my contract spell out exactly how the bonus is calculated?

Health Insurance ≠ Healthcare

Here's an important takeaway: Just because a patient has insurance doesn't mean their care will be covered.

Prior authorizations, denials, and billing errors can be daily headaches for you and your patients. The middleman (insurance companies) complicates what should be a simple doctor-patient relationship.

There's also a quiet truth that often gets lost in all the talk about networks and plans: **Cash is still an option.** Before insurance companies took center stage, patients simply paid their doctors directly. Today, many physicians (and patients) have been so overwhelmed and conditioned by the system that they forget this is still possible. You don't have to structure every service through an insurance contract. Direct payment—whether as a primary model or for selected services—remains a viable, sometimes simpler path for both you and your patients.

Where the Money Goes (Hint: Not All to You)

Let's visualize the flow:

1. You see a patient and document the visit.
2. The biller codes the encounter and submits a claim.
3. The insurer reviews, pays a portion, and sometimes denies or delays payment.
4. The practice collects what it can, writes off the rest, and pays you your share.

Figure 3: *This visual is a reminder that every dollar you help generate does not flow straight into your pocket. Between your visit and your paycheck, the claim is coded, sent to the insurer, partially paid (or denied), and then filtered through the practice's overhead and write-offs. By the time it reaches you, several layers have already taken a slice.*

Healthcare ≠ Health Insurance

Here's a distinction that gets lost all the time: Healthcare and health insurance are not the same thing. Healthcare is a service—what you actually do for patients, whether it's a checkup, a surgery, or a late-night phone call. Health insurance, on the other hand, is a financial product—a tool to help cover or offset the cost of that care. Just because someone has insurance doesn't mean they'll actually get the care they need, and just because you provide care doesn't mean you'll get paid for it.

Health insurance is built on a risk-sharing model. The idea is to pool everyone's money (via premiums) so that when someone faces a big, unexpected medical bill, the cost is spread out. But remember, insurance companies are, first and foremost, for-profit businesses. They are traded on the stock exchange. Their executives are rewarded for improving the bottom line. Their job is to manage their companies' own financial risk and return—which often means they're looking for ways to delay, deny, or underpay for care whenever possible.

Insurance as the Third Wheel

It wasn't always this complicated. Back in the day, a patient would see their doctor, pay them directly, and walk out with a receipt and a prescription. Now? There's almost always an insurance company in the middle, calling the shots.

They:

- Set the prices (through contracts and fee schedules).
- Decide what counts as "medically necessary."

- Require pre-approvals (sometimes even after the fact).
- Deny claims (more often than you'd like).
- Delay payments (pretty much standard procedure).

This middleman role doesn't just slow things down—it can have a major impact on your practice's revenue and your personal paycheck. Yet most of us never learned about this side of medicine in training, and you definitely won't find it in your CPT book.

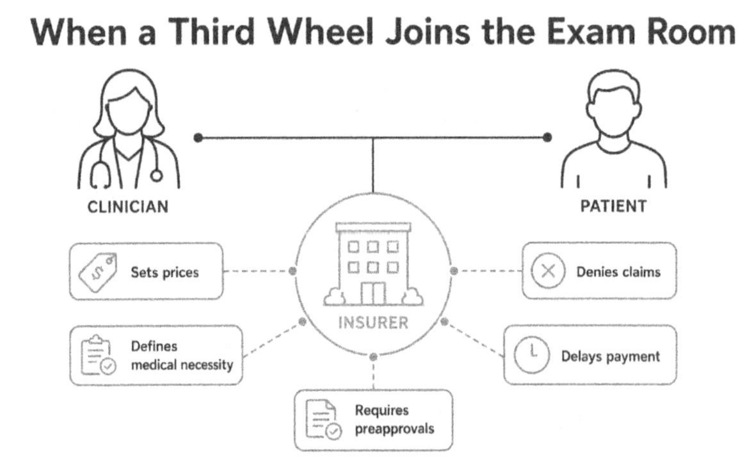

Figure 4: *This visual shows the insurer as the "third wheel" in the exam room. The clinician and patient should have a direct relationship, but the middleman sits in between, setting prices, defining "medical necessity," requiring pre-approvals, and deciding what gets denied or delayed. That extra presence doesn't just add paperwork—it shapes both the care you can give and the paycheck you ultimately receive.*

CHAPTER 6

COMPENSATION MODELS

It's What You Keep That Counts

Welcome to the financial jungle of modern medicine. You leave residency highly trained in anatomy and pharmacology, and then discover you apparently need a minor in accounting just to understand your paycheck.

If there's one subject medical schools should teach but don't, it's this: **How doctors actually get paid** and how to negotiate what you're worth. Instead, you're handed a contract, a pen, and a vague sense that you'll "figure it out."

Here's the uncomfortable truth: **Not all paychecks are created equal.** Two physicians can work just as hard, see just as many patients, and end up with very different numbers in their bank accounts. The difference isn't who's more "deserving." It's how their compensation is structured.

This chapter is meant to be a glovebox manual, not a textbook. Keep it handy when you're looking at offers, renegotiating, or just trying to figure out why your bonus looks like a rounding error.

Your Paycheck ≠ Your Value

Your salary is not a mirror of your value as a physician. It's not even a clean mirror of the revenue you generate. There's a whole Rube Goldberg machine between the care you provide and the money that hits your account.

Hospitals and large groups are designed to maximize collections and protect their margin. They are not designed to make sure every ounce of your effort shows up on your pay stub. Once you understand that, things will feel a lot less personal. In that case, ask yourself – are your economic incentives aligned with the people you are working with?

On paper, you'll show up in one of two ways with the IRS:

- W2 employee
- 1099 independent contractor

In real life, you'll be:

- Employed by a hospital, corporate group, private practice, or academic/VA system

- Independent in your own practice
- Or working in some messy hybrid of the two

Those labels matter. But they don't tell you the thing you actually care about: **how the money flows from the patient (or payor) to the organization, and then to you.** That's where reimbursement and compensation come in.

Reimbursement Versus Compensation

This is the distinction the system hopes you never really think about.

Most of us were trained to accept this whole setup as "just how medicine works." We learned how to code, how to document, and how to survive the EMR. We did *not* learn the difference between what the system gets paid and what we get paid.

So let's fix that in three sentences:

Reimbursement = what the insurer or payor pays the practice or hospital for the care you provide; this typically is not revealed to you.

Compensation = what you personally take home for doing that work.

The distance between those two numbers is where a lot of resentment lives.

Reimbursement is a **system number**. It's set by contracts, RVUs (we'll talk about this in a second), fee schedules, Medicare rules, and cost-containment strategies. It exists to control spending, not to honor your service.

Compensation is a **choice**. It's whatever formula your employer uses to chop up that revenue and decide how much goes to overhead, how much goes to administrators, and how much goes to you.

If you continue to think of reimbursement as a measure of your worth, you will always be underpaid.

Relative Value Units

Relative Value Units (RVUs) are a good example of this. They're not a score of how talented or caring you are; they're just a standardized way for Medicare and insurers to rank one visit or procedure against another so they can plug it into a payment formula. Each CPT code gets assigned a certain number of RVUs—usually broken down into work RVUs (wRVUs), practice expense RVUs (peRVUs), and malpractice RVUs (mRVUs)—based on the time, intensity, and risk involved. The payor then multiplies the total RVUs by a dollar "conversion factor" to decide how much to pay the practice for that service—not how much to pay you.

Hidden Pay Influences

There's another hidden side to all this that's easy to overlook when you're focused on working hard and "hitting your numbers": Your bottom line is affected by other people's efforts, not just your own. Your compensation can rise or fall based on how accurately someone else codes your visits, how quickly the billing team submits and follows up on claims, or how often payors deny and delay payment. That's why it's important to know what rights you have to **review and audit** the numbers being used to calculate your pay—who generates the reports, how often they're updated, and whether you're allowed to see the same data and question it if something doesn't add up.

Here's how this shows up in real life:

- If you're on a **straight salary**, you may never see a reimbursement number. But you still feel its impact. Somewhere, someone is looking at what you bring in versus what you cost. If those numbers don't make sense to them, your contract won't be renewed, or your "protected time" will quietly disappear.
- If you're on a **productivity or RVU-based model**, you live in that gap every day. You see the patients. The practice sees the payor mix. Your contract sees a formula.

This is how you end up at the end of the year thinking, *I was busy every single day—how is this bonus that small?*

Ask me how I know.

Early in my career, I assumed exactly what you probably assume: *If I work hard, fill my schedule, do good medicine, and "generate revenue," the bonus will reflect that.* It didn't.

What I eventually learned was this: Many of the patients routed to me had lower reimbursement plans or were on plans that paid a flat amount per patient (sometimes referred to as capitated), no matter how much care they required. I could work harder and harder and barely move the financial needle—not because my work lacked value, but because reimbursement on that panel was terrible.

That's the moment the lightbulb went on: The problem wasn't my effort. It was the model.

Turning This Into Something Useful

You don't need to memorize billing manuals. You do need a handful of practical questions you can ask any time someone hands you an offer.

Whenever you're looking at a job (or trying to make sense of your current one), start here:

1. Follow the money.
    - How does this practice actually get paid? Fee-for-service only? Capitated contracts? "Value-based" bonuses? A mix?
    - Translation: Is there real revenue tied to the work I'm being asked to do?
2. Find out how the pie gets sliced.
    - How is physician compensation determined here—straight salary, RVUs, collections, base + bonus, partnership?
    - Is my pay based on RVUs, collections, or just showing up?
3. Ask about the specific math for you. If RVUs are involved:
    - What is the dollar amount per wRVU in my contract?
    - Is there a threshold I need to hit before that rate applies?
    - What did the average physician in my specialty here earn last year under this model?

4. Ask who controls the levers.
    - Who controls my schedule and new patient flow?
    - Will I inherit an existing panel, or am I growing from zero?
    - Who decides which patients I see—by payor, case type, or call schedule?
5. Get real-world outcomes, not just theory.
    - How many physicians here hit their bonus last year?
    - What does a typical total compensation range look like for someone in my role after year one? After year three?

You are not being "difficult" by asking these questions. You are doing basic due diligence on a potential six-figure decision.

Keep this summary in your head:

- **Reimbursement** is how the system pays the practice.
- **Compensation** is how the practice pays you.

The less you know about the space in between, the easier for you to be underpaid.

The Most Common Compensation Models (With Real-World Translation)

You'll see lots of fancy language in contracts, but most physician compensation boils down to a few basic models or some mash-up of them.

1. Straight Salary

You get a fixed amount. Do great work, do mediocre work—same check.

Where you see it: academic centers, VA, some nonprofits, some hospital-employed jobs.

Why do some doctors like it:

- Predictable. You can plan your life.
- Less mental pressure to chase volume.

Why do some doctors end up frustrated:

- No financial recognition for staying late, adding on patients, or handling the complex cases while someone else coasts.
- Easy to become the "dumping ground" because you're not rewarded for saying yes, but you're punished informally for saying no.

When you read a straight salary offer, ask:

- Is there a review after year one or two, or is this number frozen?
- Are there informal productivity expectations even though this is "just salary"?
- Are there any bonus opportunities at all? If so, based on what?

2. Productivity-Based / RVU / Collections ("Eat What You Kill")

Here, your income depends heavily on your output. That can be measured by collections, charges, or more commonly wRVUs (work RVUs).

Where you see it: private practice, many hospital-employed roles, procedural specialties.

What sounds good:

- If you're efficient, motivated, and have good support, you can do very well.
- There is at least a theoretical link between "I worked more" and "I got paid more."

What you need to watch:

- If the practice doesn't feed you patients, or the payor mix is poor, or the thresholds are unrealistic, you'll feel like you're sprinting in quicksand.
- Volume obsession can creep into your clinical decision-making and your life outside work.

When you read a productivity offer, ask:

- What is the wRVU rate in my contract?
- What is the annual wRVU target for full pay or for a bonus?
- How does that compare to what physicians here actually hit?
- Who controls referrals and new patient distribution?

- What happens if I don't hit the target—is my base cut, or is it just less bonus?

If the answers are vague, assume the risk is on you.

3. Base + Bonus

You get a guaranteed base salary plus potential bonus for hitting certain targets: RVUs, quality metrics, patient satisfaction, or some Frankenstein combination of all three.

This is the "we'll keep you calm with a floor, then motivate you with a carrot" model.

What's nice:

- You're not fully exposed if volume dips.
- There is at least some upside if you perform well.

Where it goes sideways:

- The bonus criteria are often muddy, constantly changing, or based on metrics you don't fully control.
- Doctors hear "up to $50,000 in bonus" and mentally add that to their base, then discover three years later that no one ever actually hits $50,000.

When you read a base + bonus offer, ask:

- Exactly which metrics determine my bonus?
- Is there a cap?
- How many physicians in my department hit the full bonus last year?

- How often are bonuses calculated and paid?
- What happens if there are staffing issues, EMR changes, or other factors I can't control that affect those metrics?

If they can't give you simple, concrete examples, consider the bonus "aspirational" at best.

4. Partnership Track

You start employed, then have the option to "buy in" after a few years and become a partner/owner in the practice.

What's appealing:

- You share in profits, not just salary.
- You have a real say in how the practice is run.
- Long term, this can be one of the best paths to both autonomy and income.

What's less glamorous:

Those first few years may pay less than other offers.

The buy-in number can be vague, large, and emotionally loaded.

In some groups, "partnership track" is code for "we'll keep you dangling indefinitely."

When you're evaluating a partnership track, ask:

- What is the typical time frame to partnership, and how many people actually make it?

- What's the current buy-in, and what exactly am I buying?
- Can I see blinded numbers for what current partners actually take home?
- Once I'm a partner, how are profits distributed?

If they won't show you numbers, the answer is no—you just won't see it until it's too late.

Final Thought: Don't Be Afraid to Be "That Doctor"

You are not greedy or ungrateful when you ask about reimbursement, compensation, RVUs, bonuses, or partnership. You're being a professional.

Nobody is going to care more about your financial future than you do. They shouldn't. That's your job.

If you take nothing else from this chapter, take this:

Before you sign, make sure you understand not just **what** you're being paid, but **how** and **why**.

Once you see the structure clearly, you can decide if it's a game that you're willing to play—or whether it's time to start building something that aligns better with your values and your life.

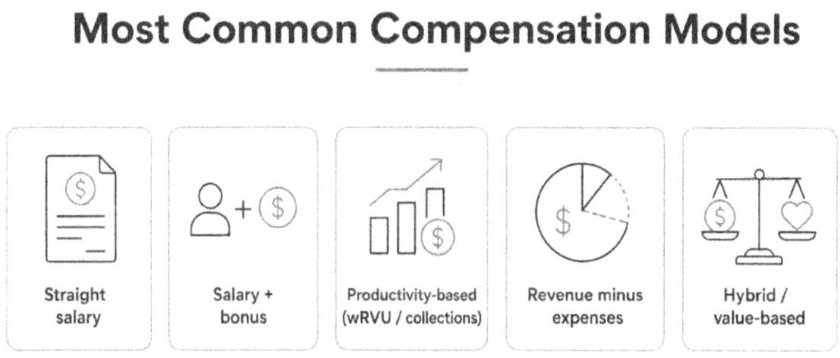

Figure 5: *This chart is a quick snapshot of how different compensation models split stability, risk, and upside. On one end, straight salary and salary-plus-bonus keep things simple and predictable. As you move right, productivity, revenue-minus-expenses, and hybrid/value-based models tie more of your income to what you produce, how efficiently the practice runs, and how well your patients do—which can increase both your opportunities and your exposure.*

SECTION TWO WRAP-UP

DOCTOR DO ✔

- ☑ **Do understand your employment model.** Know whether you're W2, 1099, or some combination—and what that means for taxes, benefits, risk, and autonomy. Be clear on whether you're an employee, an independent contractor, or on a path to partnership/ownership.

- ☑ **Do learn who actually pays you—and how.** Understand the mix of Medicare, Medicaid, TRICARE/VA, commercial insurers, cash, and any direct-pay models in your practice. Know that reimbursement is driven by contracts and fee schedules, not just "what you bill."

- ☑ **Do follow the money from payor to paycheck.** Trace how a service becomes revenue: coding, claim submission, allowed amount, adjustments, collections, overhead, and then your compensation. Notice where money leaks out (denials, write-offs, inefficiencies) before it ever reaches you.

- ☑ **Do know your compensation formula.** Make sure you can explain—in plain language—how your pay is calculated: salary, bonus, RVUs, collections, quality metrics, or some blend. Ask for examples and run a few scenarios: "If I see X more patients or add Y procedures, what changes for me?"

- ☑ **Do know your rights to see and question the numbers.** Find out what access you have to reports on RVUs, collections, and productivity, and how often they're updated. Clarify whether you can review, question, or audit those figures, especially if bonuses or penalties are tied to them.

DOCTOR DON'T ✖

- **Don't assume all physician jobs are financially equivalent.** Two positions with the same "salary" can yield very different take-home pay depending on payor mix, overhead, and how bonuses are structured.

- **Don't confuse reimbursement to the practice with compensation to you.** A higher billed or collected amount doesn't automatically mean a higher paycheck. If the formula doesn't share the upside, extra work may mostly benefit someone else.

- **Don't ignore fine print in bonus plans.** Vague language about "productivity," "incentives," or "discretionary bonuses" can hide moving targets. If you can't calculate it, you can't count on it.

- **Don't forget how dependent you are on other people's work.** Your income can be affected by coding errors, billing delays, front-desk issues, and payor behavior. Pretending it's "all on you" hides systemic problems you should at least be aware of.

- **Don't let the system define value for you by default.** Just because a metric is easy to measure (RVUs, visits per day, portal messages answered) doesn't mean it reflects the kind of medicine you want to practice.

WHY IT MATTERS

How the system pays—and how your job plugs into that system—quietly shapes your daily life. It influences how many patients you're expected to see, how long you have with each one, what kinds of visits are encouraged or discouraged, and how much freedom you have to experiment with different practice models. If you don't understand the rules of the financial game, you're more likely to feel blindsided by your paycheck, trapped in misaligned expectations, or pressured into productivity targets that don't honor your values.

When you do understand these mechanics, you can negotiate more intelligently, choose jobs and practice models that fit you, and design compensation arrangements that support your long-term autonomy instead of eroding it.

PUTTING IT INTO PRACTICE

You don't have to become a health economist. You do need a working map. Over the next few weeks, pick a few of these steps:

1. **Map your current (or future) employment model.** Write down whether the role you're considering is W2 or 1099, who "owns" the patients, and whether there's a path to partnership or ownership. Note what that means for taxes, benefits, and risk.
2. **Ask three simple money questions about any job offer:**
   a. Who are the main payors in this practice (Medicare, Medicaid, commercial, cash/direct)?
   b. How is my compensation determined (salary only, salary + RVU/collections, pure productivity)?
   c. How often will I see the reports that back this up?

3. **Request a sample compensation calculation.** Before signing, ask for a few concrete examples: "What would my total compensation look like at X RVUs/collections? At Y?" If they can't show you, that's information.

4. **Trace one "dollar of revenue" from start to finish.** Sit down with a trusted biller, administrator, or mentor and say, "Walk me through what happens to a single office visit—from the moment I see the patient until the money lands in the practice account." Notice how many steps, hands, and delays are involved.

5. **Write one non-negotiable about how you want to be paid.** For example: "I will not sign a contract where I can't see the data used to calculate my bonus," or "If I'm paid on productivity, I need protected time for non-RVU work (teaching, admin, leadership)."

These are not just financial exercises. They are part of taking informed ownership of your career—so the system doesn't quietly make decisions for you that you never consciously agreed to.

SECTION THREE

CAREER & LIFE ON YOUR TERMS

CHAPTER SEVEN

PRACTICE MODELS

Choose Your Own Adventure

How You Work Shapes Who You Become

By now, you've learned that not all jobs are created equally even when they look the same on paper. We talked earlier about employment models: who pays you, who withholds your taxes, and what kind of leash you're on (if any). But there's another layer under all of that. A quieter, deeper layer.

The structure of your work—your personal practice model—doesn't just affect your paycheck. It shapes your schedule, your stress levels, your sense of purpose, and, to some extent, your whole identity. This chapter is where we zoom out. Less about contracts and forms.

More about frameworks and freedom. About the shape your work life takes, and how much say you have over that shape.

Now, let's imagine...

You're finishing up residency. You think the hardest part is over. You've survived sleepless nights of being on call. You've excised foreign bodies and sutured incisions together. You've memorized enough billing codes to make a grown auditor weep. But then comes the real question—the one no one has really prepared you for:

How do I want to practice medicine?

It's like being handed the keys to six completely different vehicles, blindfolded, and told to pick one for a cross-country trip. Do you want speed? Comfort? Off-road capability? Good luck.

There's one job offer with a stable salary and benefits. A different one with crazy high pay but no PTO. A third one where you could build something of your own—but have to handle payroll, rent, and buy your own tongue depressors.

Each one is considered a "doctor job." But they are worlds apart.

That's what this chapter is about: not what kind of doctor you want to be—but what kind of life you want to build with medicine as your medium.

The Architecture of Autonomy

Let's look at two residents: Sam and Indie. Same graduation date. Same board scores. Same general vibe. Five years later, you wouldn't know they came from the same universe.

Sam took a job at a large academic medical center. Structured hours, research opportunities, and a solid benefits package. He loves teaching med students and enjoys the prestige of being part of a major institution. But he sometimes feels like a cog in a very large machine. EMRs get switched with little warning. Admins set productivity targets without asking physicians. He once got scolded for not meeting visit quotas—on a week when he was out with pneumonia.

Indie, on the other hand, decided to open her own primary care clinic in a mid-sized town. She sees fewer patients, takes long appointments, and knows each patient by name (and many of their dogs). There's no billing staff—because there's no insurance billing at all. Her patients pay a monthly membership fee that covers everything. She says she's never been happier... except during tax season. That's when the spreadsheets start whispering in ominous tones.

What's the difference here?

Both Sam and Indie work full time. Both care deeply. Both are board-certified and competent. But they're living different lives because they chose different practice models. Not better or worse. Just fundamentally different approaches to how medicine is delivered—and what the doctor's role looks like within that system.

Beyond Employed vs. Independent

In the earlier chapter about employment models, we laid the groundwork with W2 versus 1099 tax filings, academic versus corporate. But that's just the outer layer. This chapter is about what happens when you look inside the walls of those systems.

In each case, the job title might be "Physician," but the role you actually play—from decision-maker to employee number 457A—varies wildly.

The question isn't just: Who pays you?

It's also:

- How much control do you have?
- How is value measured in your day-to-day work?
- Who decides what success looks like in your clinic?

And underneath all of that: Does this model let you live out the values you identified back in Chapter One—or does it quietly push against them?

Designing Your Medical Life

Practice models live on a kind of spectrum—between control and risk.

On one end, there's full employment in a large system. Steady, predictable, secure. Someone else handles the logistics. But in this arrangement you could feel distant from decision-making, pressured to meet metrics you didn't create, and limited in how you care for patients.

On the other end is pure autonomy: building your own clinic, your own way. Direct care. Concierge. Micropractices. Freedom to innovate. But with freedom comes business ownership, overhead, and uncertainty.

In between, there's everything from locum tenens (where you rent your skills out temporarily) to group practices (where you're on track to co-own the shop someday). There are telemedicine jobs with flexibility and specialty cash-pay clinics that skip insurance entirely.

The key is realizing this isn't just about choosing a job. It's about crafting a practice that matches your values. If you crave structure and support, a hospital-employed role might be perfect—for now. If you burn out on bureaucracy, you might shift to a cash-based model where you call the shots. If you're just exploring your options, locums can give you a taste of multiple systems without long-term commitment.

There's No One Right Path—Just the One That Fits Right Now

Let's go back to that original question: *Where do you see yourself in five years?*

Here's the secret: Most of us don't know. And that's okay.

The truth is, these models aren't locked boxes. Many physicians move between them during their careers. You can start in an academic center, transition to group private practice, and later open a concierge clinic. Or take a sabbatical year doing locums in different states. Or start a Direct Care side gig while working part-time in urgent care.

What matters is that you know these options exist. That you're not stuck in one model forever. And that every choice—every risk and reward—is a part of the adventure you get to design.

You don't have to get it "perfect" the first time. You do have to stay awake to what fits you now, and be willing to adjust when your values, your life, or your energy tell you it's time for a different kind of practice.

CHAPTER EIGHT

CONTRACTS & NEGOTIATIONS

Psst! It's Worth Asking

The first time I opened a physician employment contract, I thought my blood pressure monitor might explode. It read like the kind of document you'd sign before going into space or entering the witness protection program. Legalese, HR jargon, and oddly vague promises, all neatly arranged in twenty pages of 10-point font. And yet, I was expected to sign it in exchange for little more than a handshake and a "Congrats, you got the job."

It was like trying to interpret an EKG while someone spins you in a swivel chair . . . fast . . . and in the dark.

Here's what I wish someone had told me from the beginning: A contract is not a sacred text. It's a conversation starter.

Somewhere along the way, rising physicians absorbed the idea that they should feel lucky just to get an offer. That asking for more is rude. That requesting clarity is somehow being ungrateful. But none of that is true. That kind of thinking diminishes your standing. Let me reframe it for you. Your contract isn't just a formal agreement. It's a mirror. It reflects the boundaries, expectations, protections, and priorities of the job.

And if you don't know how to read it, then you don't know what it says, and you're basically signing your life over blindfolded.

The Real Anatomy of a Contract

Underneath all the boilerplate language, most contracts are built from the same bones:

- How you'll be paid
- What's expected of you
- What happens if it all falls apart

But don't be fooled by how familiar the categories look. "Compensation" might not mean just your salary—it could include performance bonuses tied to RVUs you don't understand yet. "Collections" might sound generous until you realize your pay depends not only on your own work, but also on how well someone else codes, submits, tracks, and collects the money. "Call responsibilities" might sound manageable until you realize "shared equally" means you're taking every third night with a group of five . . . that only has two other full-time docs.

Here is one of the hidden sides of compensation that deserves more attention. Your bottom line can be impacted by the performance (or lack thereof) of other people. If coding is sloppy, if claims are submitted late, if denials are not appealed properly, or if the billing department is inefficient, you may feel that in your paycheck even if you've done everything right clinically. That's why it matters to know not just how your compensation is calculated, but what rights you have to review the numbers behind it. Can you see the reports? How often? Can you question them? Can you audit them if something doesn't add up?

When it comes to contracts, the devil is not in the details—it *is* the details.

Because when push comes to shove, there will come a moment when the real question is: ***What are you going to do about it?*** If your numbers look wrong, if your bonus doesn't match the formula, if your schedule quietly changes, if your call burden grows, or if your employer starts interpreting the contract in a way that somehow always benefits them, what is your remedy? Do you have the right to review the data? Do you have someone outside the employer—an attorney, accountant, or advisor—you can talk to? Does the contract spell out how disputes are handled: informally, through mediation, through arbitration, or only through expensive legal action?

You will want as much clarity on these aspects of your contract as possible:

- Malpractice coverage

- Tail insurance
- Non-compete clauses that make entire zip codes off limits after you leave
- Bonus formulas that sound precise until you try to reverse-engineer them
- Productivity metrics that depend on data you may never actually get to see
- Dispute resolution language that seems boring—until it's the only thing standing between you and being steamrolled

It's all in there. And if it isn't written down, assume it doesn't exist. "We'll figure it out later" is the employment equivalent of "Trust me, I've got you." Nice words. But not legally binding.

Learning to Read Between the Lines

Some red flags aren't red until you know what to look for. And this is exactly why you want a healthcare contract attorney reviewing all of this with you. Not because you're incapable of reading your own contract, but because you don't know what you haven't been trained to spot. A good attorney knows where the traps usually live and can help you see around corners before you sign.

You may not realize that a vague productivity formula means you'll be working harder for less. Or that a collections-based bonus may leave you vulnerable to inefficiencies in billing and follow-up that have nothing to do with how well you care for patients. Or that a compensation plan tied to "net collections" might quietly make you absorb the consequences of payor denials, write-offs, front-desk errors, and coding mistakes made by other people in the system.

You may not realize that a “termination without cause” clause with only thirty days’ notice could leave you unemployed and uninsured with barely a month to find new work. Or that a non-compete radius of forty-five miles might box you out of an entire metro area—just for deciding to leave a toxic practice.

And here’s another thing to look for: transparency. If your pay is tied to RVUs, collections, or quality metrics, the contract should make clear how those numbers are tracked, how often they are reported, and whether you have the right to review or question the underlying data. If they can use the numbers to judge your performance and calculate your pay, you should be able to see those numbers too. This is another place where your attorney can help you identify vague language, missing protections, or terms that sound acceptable until they are tested in real life.

You also need to know what happens when there is a disagreement. If the numbers don’t match, if your bonus calculation seems off, if your employer interprets the contract one way and you interpret it another, what happens next? Does the contract require informal discussion first? Mediation? Arbitration? Litigation? Who pays for that process? Where does it happen? Do you have any realistic ability to challenge their position, or are you effectively boxed into an expensive and one-sided process? These are not throw-away details. These are attorney-review details.

On the other hand, transparency is a green light. When compensation is clearly spelled out, when your call schedule is defined in writing, when your CME and vacation days are explicitly listed, when the bonus formula is understandable, when reporting is spelled out, and when the dispute process is clearly described, it's a signal from the employer that lets you know: *We've thought this through, and we want you to know what you're getting into.*

But here's the sneaky part: It's easy to second guess your feeling that something isn't quite right. It's easy to rationalize away your own best interest. That voice in your head starts up: *Maybe it's not that bad. Maybe I'm overreacting. Maybe asking for clarification will make them think I'm "difficult."*

Let me say this clearly: There is no award for being the "Nice Doctor" who quietly signs a bad deal. There is no medal for skipping attorney review and hoping for the best. If something affects your income, your schedule, your liability, your ability to leave, or your ability to challenge a problem when it arises, it deserves a closer look—by you and by an attorney who knows physician contracts inside and out.

Negotiation: Not a Battle, Just a Boundary Setting Session

A lot of us hear the word "negotiation" and immediately tense up. We picture a courtroom or a car dealership—some dramatic back-and-forth with dramatic ultimatums.

But in medicine, negotiation is usually far less dramatic. It's a conversation. A thoughtful one. One where both sides are simply trying to align expectations.

The employer wants you to succeed—burnout doesn't help their bottom line. You want a job that won't make you regret your career. That's not a stand-off. That's a shared goal.

You don't have to fight for every bullet point. Instead, choose your top priorities—maybe it's fewer call shifts, more CME money, a signing bonus that actually makes relocating viable, or clearer language around how your compensation will be measured and reported—and advocate for those. You're not being greedy. You're advocating for the life you want to live outside of work.

And if your pay is tied to productivity, collections, or incentives, don't be afraid to ask practical questions:

- Who generates the reports?
- How often are they updated?
- What data will you have access to?
- Do you have the right to review or challenge the numbers if something seems off?

Those are not rude questions. They are professional questions.

Most employers won't blink. Some will even respect you more. And if they don't? If they act insulted or try to guilt you for asking? That's not a missed opportunity. That's a dodged bullet.

Calling In a Pro

(And Why Your Cousin the Real Estate Lawyer Doesn't Count)

Even the most meticulous physician can miss a legal landmine hidden in a sentence. That's why, if there's ever a time to outsource expertise, this is it.

Find a healthcare contract attorney. Not someone who "does contracts sometimes," but someone who eats, sleeps, and breathes physician agreements. They'll spot the clauses you've never heard of, translate the legalese into plain English, and often help you negotiate smarter, not harder.

They can also help you identify where a compensation formula looks polished on the surface but lacks the transparency or accountability you'd need to trust it. Sometimes the issue isn't the number itself. It's the inability to verify how the number was reached—or to challenge it if it looks wrong.

The cost? Often a flat fee—somewhere between a fancy dinner and a weekend getaway. The value? Potentially tens of thousands over the life of your contract—and a whole lot of peace of mind.

What I Wish Someone Had Told Me

You are not just signing a job. You are signing a lifestyle. You're agreeing to how your time will be spent, how your work will be valued, how your compensation will be calculated, and how much flexibility you'll have to grow (or leave) if the fit turns out to be wrong.

You're also stepping into a system where your paycheck may be influenced by people and processes you do not directly control. That doesn't mean you need to be suspicious of everyone. It just means you need to be awake. If your income depends on reports, formulas, billing processes, or departmental efficiency, then part of protecting yourself is making sure you understand what access and review rights you have from the outset—and getting those rights in writing.

So read every word. Ask every question. Get someone you trust to look it over with you—ideally a healthcare contract attorney whose sole job is to protect *you*. And if something feels off—ask. Push back. Clarify. You're not a problem. You're a professional.

Because the contract isn't the end of the negotiation. It's just the beginning of your boundaries.

Remember, just like in your patient notes: If it's not in writing, it doesn't count.

CHAPTER NINE

BURNOUT & BOUNDARIES

Becoming Human Again

There comes a moment in nearly every physician's medical career when you find yourself staring at the ceiling at three in the morning wondering if this is just exhaustion . . . or if your soul is quietly trying to climb out the window. You're not sick, exactly. You're not quitting, not yet. But something is definitely . . . off.

Maybe it's that sixth shift in a row. Or the inbox that never empties. Or the way your pager waits for you to enter a bathroom stall before it comes alive with shrieking purpose. Whatever the trigger, the feeling is unmistakable: You're running on fumes.

We don't talk about this enough in medicine—not in real terms. Burnout gets tossed around like a buzzword, a checkbox on a wellness survey, or something that happens to other people. But burnout is not a sign of weakness. It's a sign you've been strong for too long without refilling the tank.

And no, you're not imagining it. Even the most passionate, mission-driven physician can get crispy.

The Burnout Thermometer: Know When You're Toast

The goal isn't to live in the "Golden Brown" zone every day (Spoiler: Life doesn't work that way). The goal is to recognize when you're heating up—before you're fully burnt.

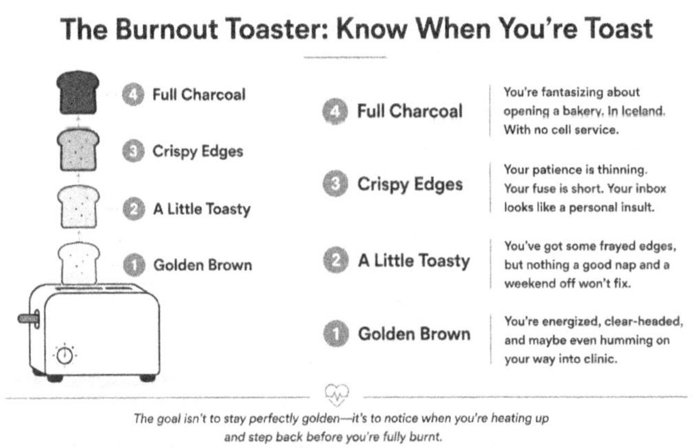

Figure 6: *The Burnout Toaster*

And here's the part that often gets missed: Your practice model, your contract, your compensation structure, and your daily workload expectations all turn the burner up or down. If you're in a setting where your value is measured only in RVUs, double-booked schedules, and portal messages answered at 10 p.m., that dial is going to be higher by default. If your contract quietly ties your pay to metrics you can't control or even see, the heat sneaks up on you faster.

The Doctor Guilt Gremlin

You know that little voice that pipes up the moment you think about taking a break? The one that whispers, you should be doing more... Your patients need you... You're falling behind...

That's the Doctor Guilt Gremlin. And it is a liar.

It tells you that asking for help is failure. That saying "no" is selfish. That you're supposed to sacrifice everything—and smile while doing it. The Gremlin thrives on shame and overwork.

But here's the truth: Rest is not laziness. Recharging is not weakness. Saying "no" to one more committee, task, or inbox "quick question" does not mean you don't care—it means you want to keep caring, without unraveling.

Sometimes the Gremlin even uses money and contracts against you: You can't say no, your bonus depends on this... You signed up for this schedule... You should be grateful you even have this job. That's why it's so important to understand your employment model and compensation up front—so you don't accidentally sign an agreement that weaponizes guilt against you later.

Boundaries: The Ultimate PPE

If masks protect your face and gloves protect your hands, then boundaries are your emotional PPE. They guard your energy, your time, and your ability to stay human. And in medicine, that's not just helpful, it's essential.

Start with this radical idea: **"No" is a complete sentence.**

You don't have to justify declining an extra shift. You don't have to give a TED Talk on why you're not checking email after 7 p.m. You can simply decide: This is where my work ends, and I begin.

Think of it like setting a fence around your most precious resource: YOU. And yes, it may feel uncomfortable at first. You're probably used to being the "yes" person, the helper, the fixer. But boundaries aren't about being difficult. They're about being sustainable.

Some of those boundaries belong in your **contract**, not just in your head. Protected time. Reasonable call expectations. Clear caps on clinic sessions or panel size. Clarity about how much "unseen" work (messages, refills, forms) is expected—and whether it's actually recognized in your compensation. The more you get in writing, the easier it will be to hold the line later without feeling like you're making it up as you go.

Physician, Heal Thyself

There's an unspoken code in medicine: You don't stop. You just keep going. Push through. Power on. You're the healer, not the one who needs help.

But that mindset is how physicians end up in the "Full Charcoal" zone. Remember this: You are not a machine. You're a human with a pulse and a psyche and needs. You can't practice medicine effectively if you're chronically depleted.

That means doing the hard (but necessary) thing: checking in with yourself regularly. It might be a quiet morning walk. Or a calendar block that says "DO NOT

SCHEDULE." Or a real, open conversation with a mentor, therapist, or colleague where you admit—honestly—that you're struggling.

It can also mean looking at the system you're in and asking: Is this practice model still compatible with the values I identified back in Chapter One? Is this employment arrangement—these metrics, this call schedule, this compensation plan—helping me thrive or slowly bleeding me dry?

None of this makes you broken. It makes you wise.

How to Start Taking Your Energy Seriously

A few years ago, a mentor gave me the best burnout advice I've ever heard: "Protect your energy like it's on a drip. Because it is."

Picture a pie chart or an IV bag that represents your energy for the week. Every consult, every shift, every inbox reply, every code blue pulls from that bag. If you don't refill it—sleep, joy, movement, connection—it runs dry.

Your job is important. But so is your family. Your creativity. Your weekend. Your sense of humor.

You are more than your productivity.

And remember: Some of the biggest leaks in that IV bag are structural, not personal. It's not just "I should be more resilient." It's also:

- This clinic template is unsafe.
- This RVU target is unrealistic.

- This compensation model rewards volume over sanity.
- This contract gives me no say over my schedule.

You can work on your personal habits and your system at the same time. Saying "no" to one extra shift is important. So is, at some point, choosing a practice model, contract, and compensation structure that doesn't require you to constantly sacrifice yourself to keep up.

When to Ask for Help (And What That Can Look Like)

If you're deep in the "Crispy Edges," you're not alone—and you're not stuck. Help doesn't have to mean something dramatic. It can be small, intentional actions:

- A text to a friend who gets it
- A quiet therapy session where you don't have to be "on"
- Telling your boss, "I'm at capacity and need to step back"
- Or even just blocking time on your calendar labeled, "Me"

You can also check out what's available to you—whether it's a physician wellness program, a peer support group, or just someone you trust enough to say, "Hey, I'm not okay right now."

Sometimes asking for help looks like consulting an attorney about whether you have options if the job you're in is truly unsustainable. Sometimes it looks like revisiting your contract before renewal and saying, "These expectations aren't workable for me long term. Here's what I need to stay." Sometimes it looks like changing practice models altogether.

There is no merit badge for white-knuckling your way through burnout. Vulnerability is not a liability. It's a tool. One you'll need if you want a career that doesn't chew you up and spit you out.

You are allowed to design a life in medicine that lets you be a whole human—not just a very tired pair of hands.

CHAPTER TEN

LEADERSHIP & GROWTH

Even if You Are Not in Charge

Before you ever thought about titles, committees, or "moving the needle," you probably started your journey for one simple reason: to help people—one person at a time. Not with a plaque on your desk or your name on a policy. Just by showing up, day after day, with your brain, your hands, and your heart. This is a noble start to your career and the heartbeat of the profession.

As your career progresses, however, you will begin to notice more and more the word "leadership" surfacing. It gets tangled up with job descriptions, prestige, and LinkedIn profiles. It calls to mind board positions, authorship, peer-reviewed studies. That's what I call "loud" leadership because it calls attention to you and your expertise.

But real leadership? Real leadership is quieter than that. It happens in exam rooms and break rooms. It starts with how you treat the nurse, the intern, the patient. It looks a lot less like a management seminar and a lot more like the basic rules you learned as a child: Be kind, share, say please and thank you, clean up your mess. Think of it as the Robert Fulghum *All I Really Need to Know I Learned in Kindergarten* version of leadership—applied in a white coat. And most importantly—it doesn't require a title.

Let's take this chapter to redefine leadership—not as something you eventually earn, but as something you quietly practice every day.

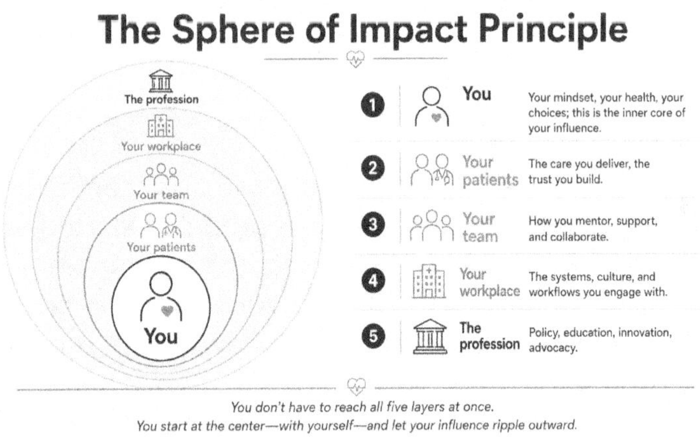

Figure 7: *The Sphere of Impact Principle*

The Sphere of Impact Principle

Think of your influence as a series of concentric circles:

- You: your mindset, your health, your choices; this is

the inner core of your influence.

- Your patients: the care you deliver, the trust you build
- Your team: how you mentor, support, and collaborate
- Your workplace: the systems, culture, and workflows you engage with
- The profession: policy, education, innovation, advocacy

You don't have to reach all five layers at once. You start at the center—with yourself—and let your influence ripple outward. When you protect your own energy, uphold your boundaries, and practice medicine in alignment with your values, you're already leading, whether you realize it or not.

And those kindergarten rules still apply as your circles expand:

- Be gentle with yourself.
- Share what you've learned.
- Don't hit back when you're frustrated—pause, breathe, and respond.
- Take responsibility when you mess up.

These simple habits, repeated, quietly shape every circle around you.

Even if your current "job" feels small, your impact doesn't have to be.

You Don't Need a Title to Lead

Some of the best leaders in medicine don't have the word "Chief" in their email signature. They're the attendings who remember what it felt like to be terrified on call. The residents who stop to teach, even when they're swamped. The students who ask the hard questions others are too afraid to raise.

Here's what untitled leadership looks like in action:

- You teach the new med student where the code cart is, even though no one asked you to.
- You speak up when a policy isn't working for patients or staff.
- You say "no" to the toxic overtime culture—and mean it.
- You model honesty, empathy, and balance—even on the rough days.

Underneath all of those actions are the same simple principles: Share what you know, include the new kid, don't hoard the good stuff for yourself, treat people the way you would want to be treated if you were the one scared, confused, or exhausted.

Real leaders don't climb the ladder by stepping on others. They lift others as they rise—and they leave a trail of stronger, more confident people behind them.

You don't have to wait for a promotion to start leading. In fact, most of the time, promotions come *after* you've already been showing up as a leader for a while.

Leadership Is a Verb, Not a Noun

It's not about being the loudest voice in the room. It's about being the steady one. The generous one. The person who asks, "How can we make this better—for the patient, for each other, for ourselves?"

Leadership is:

- What you model
- How you listen
- What you make safe for others to say
- Who you advocate for when no one's watching

Think back to those early rules: Take turns, listen, don't hog the toys, say you're sorry when you hurt someone, help clean up—even if you didn't make the mess alone. Those aren't just playground rules. They're leadership rules. They determine whether people feel safe speaking up, whether they trust you with the truth, and whether they want to work beside you when things get hard.

In medicine, leadership is often invisible—but its effects are not. A single person who consistently models respect, clarity, and healthy boundaries can shift an entire team's culture over time.

Teaching and Mentoring: The Ripple Effect

Think back to your first terrifying steps in the hospital. Someone helped you. Maybe they explained an order set. Maybe they told you where to get coffee. Maybe they just looked you in the eye and said, "You're doing okay."

Now it's your turn.

Mentorship isn't formal. It can look like:

- Sharing a mistake so others don't repeat it
- Reassuring someone that they're not the only one who's overwhelmed
- Offering perspective, encouragement, or just time

Every moment you invest in someone else multiplies. You teach one person, and they teach ten more. That's legacy. That's leadership.

In kindergarten terms: You don't push someone off the swing; you make room on the bench. You don't laugh when someone trips; you help them up. The same goes for medicine. When you choose to be the person who steadies, includes, and encourages, you change the temperature of the whole room.

Growing Yourself (So You Can Grow Others)

Medicine changes fast. Guidelines, tech, workflows, patient expectations—they're all evolving.

The best leaders stay curious.

They read. They ask questions. They stay humble. They get feedback—and actually USE it. They recognize that "I don't know yet" is not a confession of incompetence; it's a commitment to growth.

And growth isn't just about new skills. It's about perspective. Compassion. Recognizing that no matter how much you know, there's always more to learn.

As you grow, you'll start to see where your practice model,

your contract, and your environment support that growth—and where they stifle it. Leadership includes the courage to say, "This isn't working anymore," and to seek out (or create) spaces where you and your patients can thrive.

That takes the same kind of courage it took in grade school to say, "This isn't fair," or "We need to do this differently." Only now, the stakes are higher—and the impact is bigger.

Making Medicine Better (One Step at a Time)

Leadership isn't about fixing everything. It's about noticing what's broken—and doing what you can, where you are.

Maybe you:

- Streamline a confusing discharge process
- Advocate for a translator for a patient who's struggling
- Start a lunch group where residents can actually talk about burnout without shame

These things don't make headlines. But they make medicine better. Small actions, repeated, create culture. And culture is where transformation begins.

The questions are simple:

- What's not working?
- How would I want this to feel if I were on the receiving end?
- What tiny step could I take so that it feels a little more humane?

You don't have to overhaul the entire health system to lead. You can start with one hallway, one clinic, one team.

A Gentle Guide to Leadership

- **Notice what's not working:** What do people whisper about but never address?
- **Speak up:** even when your voice shakes.
- **Model balance and boundaries:** It gives others permission to do the same.
- **Lift others as you climb:** Share credit. Offer encouragement. Celebrate others' wins.
- **Stay curious:** Ask how things could be done better.
- **Be real:** Vulnerability builds trust faster than any resume ever could.
- **Practice the basics you learned early:** Be kind. Take turns. Say please and thank you. Share what you have. Say you're sorry when you're wrong. Clean up your part of the mess.

Leadership isn't a job description. It's a way of showing up. It starts with how you carry yourself on a random Tuesday. It lives in the questions you ask and the space you hold for others. And it grows every time you choose courage over comfort, generosity over ego, and curiosity over control.

You don't need a podium. You just need a voice—and the willingness to use it. And always, always remember: True leadership begins with the patient in front of you.

Leadership isn't a promotion. It's a posture. And a surprising amount of what you need to know about it, you already learned a long time ago—back in kindergarten.

Another quiet influence for me comes from *Interior Freedom* by Jacques Philippe, which makes a simple but radical point: Even when you can't control your circumstances, you can still choose your inner response. You may not always get to choose the system you work in, the policies handed down, or the pressures placed on you—but you can choose the spirit in which you show up, the way you treat others, and the freedom you guard inside your own heart. That interior freedom is where your values, your boundaries, and your leadership all meet.

As long as you keep telling yourself the truth, taking the next right step, and refusing to abandon your own humanity, there is always hope for a good life in medicine—you will bend, you will adapt, you will grow, and with each season you will discover that your calling is stronger than any one job, contract, or system.

SECTION THREE WRAP-UP

DOCTOR DO ✓

- ☑ Do treat your contract, compensation, and practice model as tools—not as verdicts on your worth.
- ☑ Do ask clear questions about money, expectations, and non-competes before you sign (or resign).
- ☑ Do keep your values and desired lifestyle in front of you when evaluating any job or practice change.
- ☑ Do give yourself permission to think creatively about how and where you practice medicine.
- ☑ Do remember that you're allowed to renegotiate, pivot, or leave when something no longer fits.
- ☑ Do protect your "intentional space" so you can think, rest, and make decisions you won't regret.

DOCTOR DON'T ✕

- Don't assume "this is just how it is" when something feels misaligned or exploitative.
- Don't outsource all the decisions about your time, energy, and income to a system that doesn't know you.
- Don't ignore red flags in contracts or culture just because you're grateful to have a job.
- Don't confuse being overextended with being indispensable.
- Don't wait until you're burned out, bitter, or desperate to explore other models or options.
- Don't forget that you are more than your wRVUs, your inbox, or your current position.

You are allowed to bring both your heart and your head to

this part of the work. The more clearly you see your options, the more courage you'll have to build a life in medicine that actually fits you—and the people you're called to serve.

WHY IT MATTERS

This is where the abstract talk about "values" slams into the concrete realities of money, contracts, and practice models. This is the part most physicians were never properly taught, which is exactly why so many end up feeling trapped, underpaid, or out of alignment with the life they actually want. When you don't understand how you're being paid, what you've signed, or what options exist outside the default employment track, it's easy to assume you have no real choices.

But you do!

Knowing how compensation works, what's buried in your contract, and how different practice models function gives you back something the system quietly erodes: a sense of agency. It lets you look at your current situation and say, "This fits me," or "This needs to change," with your eyes open. And when your external commitments begin to reflect your internal priorities, everything else in this book—boundaries, burnout prevention, leadership, even joy—gets easier to protect.

PUTTING IT INTO PRACTICE

You don't need to remake your whole career before your first paycheck. Start with one or two small, concrete moves that steer your early practice toward the values you want to protect.

You might:

- **Read your offer and contract with a highlighter.** Mark anything you don't understand or that makes you uneasy, then schedule time with a mentor, lawyer, or trusted colleague to get clear answers.
- **Draw a simple week-in-your-life chart:** clinical hours, on-call blocks, administrative time, sleep, and family commitments. Seeing it makes it obvious what you're trading for each role.
- **List your top three non-negotiables** (for example: one dinner a week with family, church on Sundays, or two evenings protected for rest) and compare them to the schedule the job really requires.
- Choose one tiny experiment for the next ninety days—a firm end-of-day cutoff, a 15-minute buffer between clinic patients, or a weekly "no admin" morning—to test how boundaries feel and what they protect.
- **Start a short "what if" file** (notes, voice memo, or doc) of alternate practice ideas—direct primary care/direct specialty care, part-time private practice, locums, or a hybrid model—so you know options exist even if you don't act on them now.

The goal is alignment, not perfection. Each honest question you ask, each clause you clarify, and each small boundary you try is an early vote for a sustainable career—and for keeping your calling intact as you grow.

CONCLUSION

After reading this book, you now see that the system is complicated, political, and often indifferent to your well-being. You also see that you are not helpless in it. You have levers you can pull: the values you choose, the employment models you consider, the contracts you sign (or don't), the boundaries you set, and the leadership you exercise. Practicing medicine can still be every bit as rewarding as you imagined — as long as you make wise professional choices along the way.

You're Not Powerless in This System!

Allow me to remind you about Options — some key Dos and Don'ts

DOCTOR DO

- ☑ Do return to your values before you say yes to any job, contract, or new role. If it doesn't fit who you are, it will cost you more than it pays.
- ☑ Do keep asking questions—about money, RVUs, payor mix, non-competes, culture, expectations—until you actually understand the answers.
- ☑ Do treat yourself and your practice as your first patient: monitor it, adjust the plan when something isn't working, and ask for help when you need it.
- ☑ Do cultivate community, mentorship, and support so you're not carrying the weight of this career alone.

DOCTOR DON'T

- Don't assume the default path is the only or "right" one just because it's what most people around you are doing.
- Don't sign away years of your life in a contract you don't understand, hoping it will all work out.
- Don't accept chronic burnout, moral injury, or misalignment as "just how medicine is."
- Don't forget that autonomy isn't anti-establishment; it's a safeguard against becoming trapped in a version of practice that harms you and, eventually, your patients.

Finally, understand that you are stepping into a profession that still holds tremendous meaning, but at the same time, beware that the system that the profession functions within is not designed to prioritize your well-being. That's why your judgment, your boundaries, and your choices matter so much.

You are your practice's first patient. If something about your career starts to feel unwell, trust your gut. You are allowed—and obligated — to notice, to reevaluate, and to adjust. That isn't selfish; it's how you preserve the capacity to care for countless others over a lifetime.

Thank you for letting this book be part of your training for the unspoken part of medicine: the part that exists outside the exam room and shapes everything that happens inside it.

You have more control than you were led to believe. Use it, thoughtfully and courageously, as you build a life in medicine that is worthy of the physician you have become.

ACKNOWLEDGEMENTS

To my family, Michael, Timothy, and Caitlyn—

Thank you for your honest feedback, steady encouragement, and for letting this project take up time, energy, and mental real estate that could have gone to a hundred other things. You kept me anchored to real life while I worked through all of this.

To my parents, Dewey & Adelaida —

You didn't just talk about "good medicine," you showed it to me day after day. As physicians, you modeled what a real doctor–patient relationship looks like: listening without rushing, treating people instead of just problems, and respecting the trust that comes with every visit. That's the picture I've carried with me into every clinic, every O.R., and every chapter of this book. The way you practiced—steady, patient focused, and honest—has given me an example to follow.

To my editor, Susan Patnaik—

Thank you for once again helping me untangle my thoughts, find the right words, and shape these ideas into something coherent and readable. From the first book to this one, your thoughtful guidance, sharp eye for detail, and well timed "this still isn't quite there yet" feedback have made my work stronger, clearer, and far more organized than it starts out in my head.

To my students and residents—

Whether you rotated through my office, sat through my lectures, or found me through various channels online, you played a bigger role in this book than you probably realize. Your curiosity, your questions, and your refusal to simply accept "that's how it is" forced me to sharpen my thinking and get clear on what actually matters in how we practice. This book is better because you chose to be active participants in your training instead of passive observers.

And finally, to every doctor who has ever thought, "There has to be a better way to do this"—

This book is for you. As you step into medicine, you will be told "this is just how it works" more times than you can count; you don't have to accept that as the only option. You have the chance to build your career around your values from the start, instead of trying to fix it later. You just need to decide you're done playing by rules that were never written for you—and start acting on it.

RESOURCES

This is not a comprehensive list; it's simply a handful of resources I've jotted down or been handed along the way. Think of them as the next layer on top of what you've already started in this book—meant to reinforce your values, sharpen your money decisions, clarify your practice options, and help you use your voice with more confidence.

You are not starting from scratch here. You're building on what you've already seen, and you still have more say in this story than the system will ever admit.

VALUES, MEANING & EMPOWERMENT

☑ **DO:** get clear on who you are and what matters before the system tells you who to become.

■ **DON'T:** build a career on drift, fear, or somebody else's definition of success.

- *How to Be a Rock Star Doctor* — Rebekah Bernard, MD
- *Sparks Start Fires* — Julie Gunther, MD
- *Living and Practicing by Design: Saving the Hearts That Care for Our Lives* — John Hayes Jr., MD
- *The Dawn*: A Med Student's Roadmap to Finding a Light in their Darkest Hour — Delicia Haynes, MD

MONEY & FINANCIAL AUTONOMY

☑ **DO:** learn enough about money early to protect your options later.

■ **DON'T:** assume financial autonomy magically shows up with an attending paycheck.

- *The White Coat Investor: A Doctor's Guide to Personal Finance and Investing* — James Dahle, MD
- *The Financially Intelligent Physician: What They Didn't Teach You in Medical School* — David Norris, MD, MBA
- *Financial Freedom Rx: The Physician's Guide to Achieving Financial Independence* — Chirag P. Shah, MD and Jayanth Sridhar, MD
- *The Doctor's Guide to Eliminating Debt* — Cory S. Fawcett, MD
- *The Physician Philosopher's Guide to Personal Finance: The 20% of Personal Finance Doctors Need to Know to Get 80% of the Results* — James Turner, MD

INDEPENDENT PRACTICE & THE BUSINESS OF MEDICINE

☑ **DO:** learn how the machine works and how physicians build practices they can shape.

■ **DON'T:** act surprised when business decisions and ownership structures shape your clinical life.

- *The Business Side of Medicine: What Medical Schools Don't Teach You* — Tom Harbin, MD, MBA
- *Business Basics for Physicians* — Texas Medical Association
- *Private Practice Solution: Reclaiming Physician Autonomy and Restoring the Doctor-Patient Relationship* — Grace Torres-Hodges, DPM, MBA
- *The Medical Entrepreneur* — Steven Hacker, MD

PODCASTS & PLATFORMS

DOCTOR DO:

☑ Listen on purpose. Choose one or two shows and treat them like a minicurriculum, not background noise.

☑ Use what you hear to learn how money, business models, and policy actually shape your day-to-day work.

☑ Capture one concrete takeaway per episode—a term to look up, a question to ask, or a step to try this month.

DOCTOR DON'T:

■ Reduce your education to grades, boards, and match lists while ignoring how the system around you function.

■ Stay in a physician-only bubble and assume "somebody else" will handle the business and policy side for you.

- AHealthcareZ by Dr. Eric Bricker
- Becker's Healthcare Podcast
- Benjamin Rush Institute
- Docs Outside the Box with Dr. Nii Darko
- Dr. Glaucomflecken by Dr. Will Flanary
- The EntreMD Podcast with Dr. Nneka Unachukwu (aka Dr Una)
- Healthcare Americana
- KevinMD with Dr. Kevin Pho
- Physician on FIRE
- SoMeDocs with Dr. Dana Coriel
- White Coat Investor Podcast

ABOUT THE AUTHOR

Dr. Grace Torres-Hodges is a board-certified podiatrist and foot surgeon in solo private practice, serving the Gulf Coast communities surrounding Pensacola, Florida, since 2001. She completed her undergraduate studies at Vanderbilt University, earned her Doctor of Podiatric Medicine from the New York College of Podiatric Medicine, and holds an MBA from the Quantic School of Business and Technology. She completed her residency in podiatric medicine and surgery at St. Vincent's Medical Center and has served on the surgical staff of the Andrews Institute for Orthopedics & Sports Medicine.

Dr. Torres-Hodges has taught medical students and residents through the Florida State University College of Medicine and military-affiliated training programs at Naval Hospital Pensacola and Eglin Air Force Base. She is the award-winning author of *Private Practice Solution*—recipient of the 2024 Independent Press Award for Medicine and the 2024 International Impact Award for Business—and a recognized advocate for physician autonomy, independent private practice, and the doctor–patient relationship.

If this book spoke to you, thank you for being here.

If this book gave you even a little clarity, comfort, or courage, I'd be grateful if you'd pass that along.

Leave a review online,
Share it with someone who may need it, or
Simply start the conversation.

Sometimes, the smallest act of sharing can reach farther than we realize.

Thank you for reading.

www.ingramcontent.com/pod-product-compliance
Lightning Source LLC
LaVergne TN
LVHW022223200926
848481LV00006B/2094
9798989170746